Iran in World History

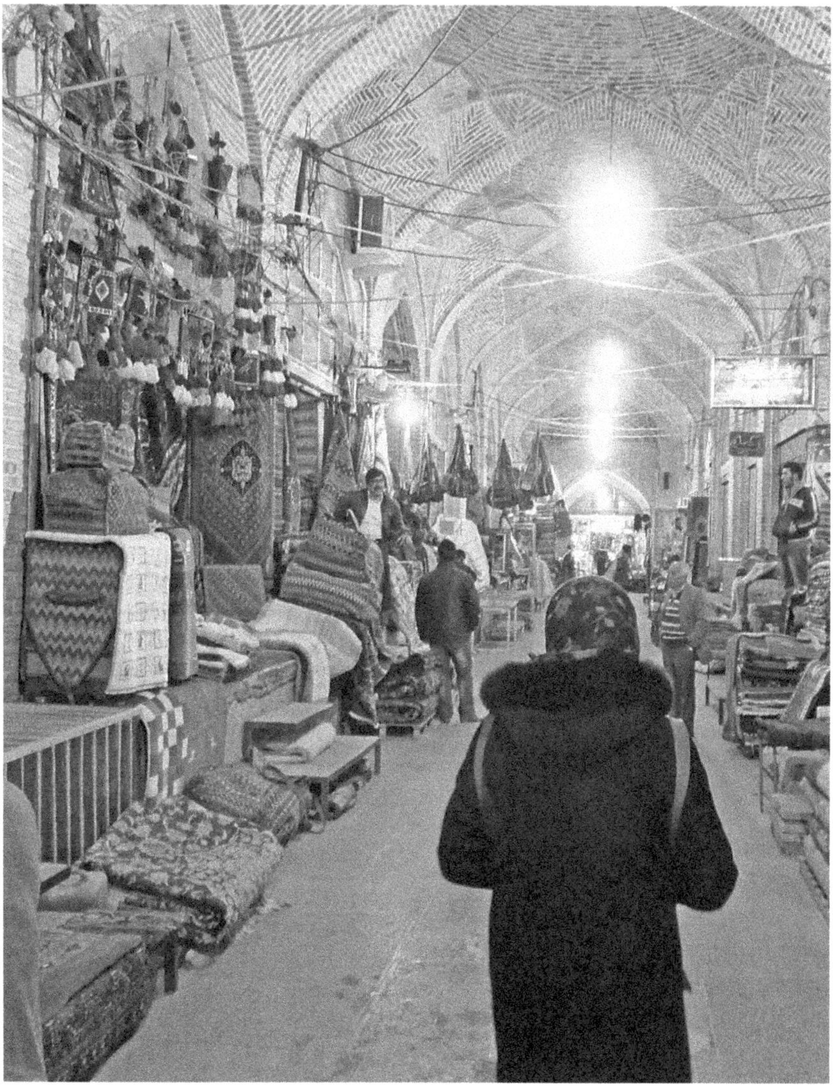

The New Oxford World History

Iran in World History

Richard Foltz

OXFORD
UNIVERSITY PRESS

OXFORD
UNIVERSITY PRESS

Oxford University Press is a department of the University of
Oxford. It furthers the University's objective of excellence in research,
scholarship, and education by publishing worldwide.

Oxford   New York
Auckland   Cape Town   Dar es Salaam   Hong Kong   Karachi
Kuala Lumpur   Madrid   Melbourne   Mexico City   Nairobi
New Delhi   Shanghai   Taipei   Toronto

With offices in
Argentina   Austria   Brazil   Chile   Czech Republic   France   Greece
Guatemala   Hungary   Italy   Japan   Poland   Portugal   Singapore
South Korea   Switzerland   Thailand   Turkey   Ukraine   Vietnam

Oxford is a registered trademark of Oxford University Press
in the UK and certain other countries.

Published in the United States of America by
Oxford University Press
198 Madison Avenue, New York, NY 10016

© Oxford University Press 2016

All rights reserved. No part of this publication may be reproduced, stored in
a retrieval system, or transmitted, in any form or by any means, without the prior
permission in writing of Oxford University Press, or as expressly permitted by law,
by license, or under terms agreed with the appropriate reproduction rights organization.
Inquiries concerning reproduction outside the scope of the above should be sent to the
Rights Department, Oxford University Press, at the address above.

You must not circulate this work in any other form
and you must impose this same condition on any acquirer.

Library of Congress Cataloging-in-Publication Data
Foltz, Richard, 1961–
Iran in world history / Richard Foltz.
pages cm. — (New Oxford world history)
Includes bibliographical references and index.
ISBN 978–0–19–933549–7 (pbk. : alk. paper) —
ISBN 978–0–19–933550–3 (hardcover : alk. paper)
1. Iran—History. 2. World history. I. Title.
DS272.F65 2015
955—dc23
2015006891

1 3 5 7 9 8 6 4 2
Printed in the United States of America
on acid-free paper

Front cover: Rostam, the hero of Ferdowsi's tenth-century epic poem the Book of Kings, *fights the White Demon, depicted in glazed tiles above the entryway to the Karim Khan Zand citadel, eighteenth century, Shiraz.* Photo by Manya Saadi-nejad

Frontispiece: Vakil bazaar, Shiraz. Photo by author

To Manya

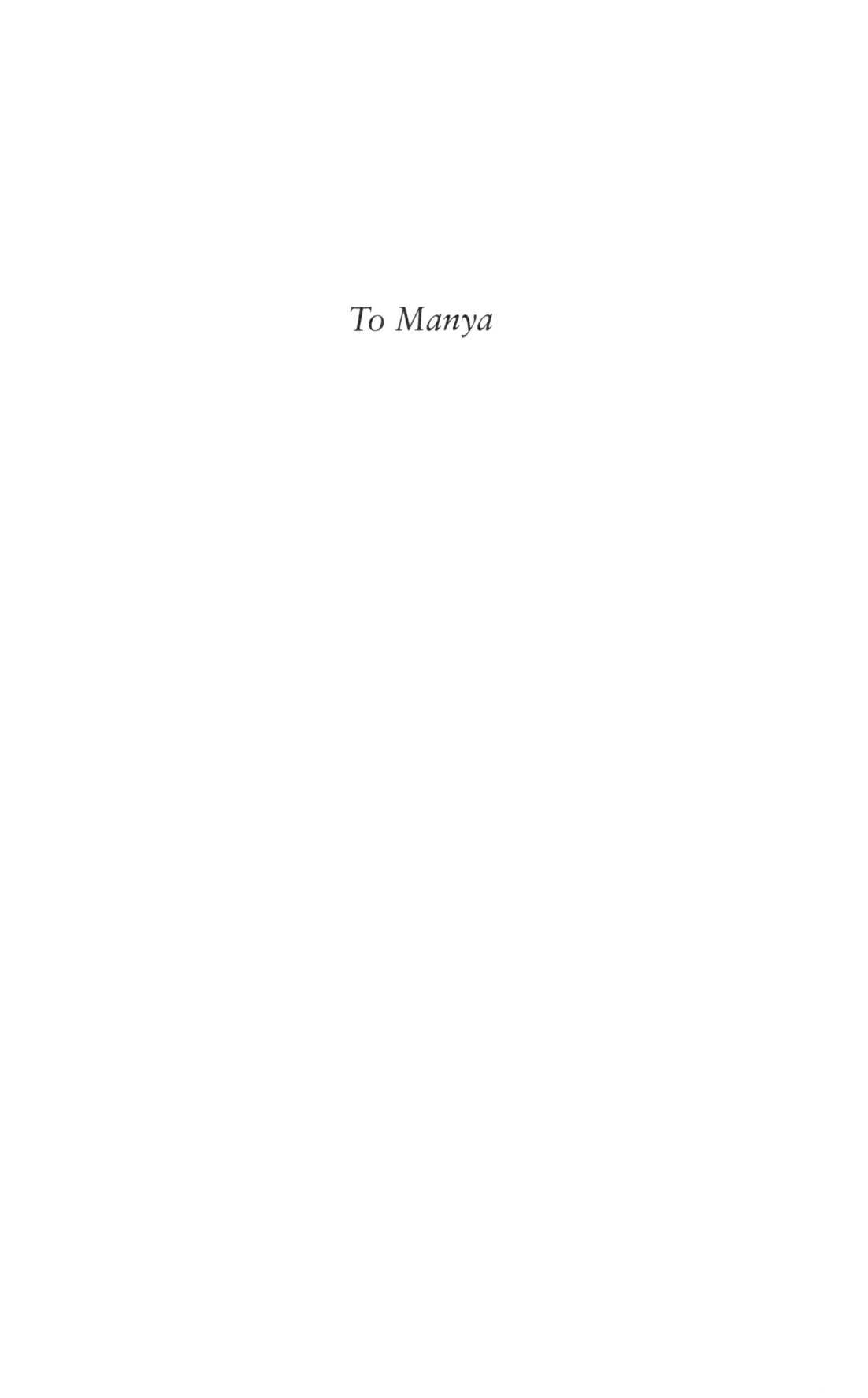

Contents

Editors' Preface ix

Preface xi

CHAPTER 1 A Convergence of Land and Language
(3500–550 BCE) 1

CHAPTER 2 Iran and the Greeks (550–247 BCE) 15

CHAPTER 3 Parthians, Sasanians, and Sogdians
(247 BCE–651 CE) 29

CHAPTER 4 The Iranization of Islam (651–1027) 45

CHAPTER 5 The Turks: Empire-Builders and Champions
of Persian Culture (1027–1722) 60

CHAPTER 6 Under Europe's Shadow (1722–1925) 80

CHAPTER 7 Modernization and Dictatorship: The Pahlavi
Years (1925–1979) 96

CHAPTER 8 The Islamic Republic of Iran (1979–present) 110

Chronology 125

Notes 127

Further Reading 131

Websites 135

Acknowledgments 137

Index 143

Editors' Preface

This book is part of the New Oxford World History, an innovative series that offers readers an informed, lively, and up-to-date history of the world and its people that represents a significant change from the "old" world history. Only a few years ago, world history generally amounted to a history of the West—Europe and the United States—with small amounts of information from the rest of the world. Some versions of the "old" world history drew attention to every part of the world *except* Europe and the United States. Readers of that kind of world history could get the impression that somehow the rest of the world was made up of exotic people who had strange customs and spoke difficult languages. Still another kind of "old" world history presented the story of areas or peoples of the world by focusing primarily on the achievements of great civilizations. One learned of great buildings, influential world religions, and mighty rulers but little of ordinary people or more general economic and social patterns. Interactions among the world's peoples were often told from only one perspective.

This series tells world history differently. First, it is comprehensive, covering all countries and regions of the world and investigating the total human experience—even those of so-called peoples without histories living far from the great civilizations. "New" world historians thus share in common an interest in all of human history, even going back millions of years before there were written human records. A few "new" world histories even extend their focus to the entire universe, a "big history" perspective that dramatically shifts the beginning of the story back to the big bang. Some see the "new" global framework of world history today as viewing the world from the vantage point of the Moon, as one scholar put it. We agree. But we also want to take a closeup view, analyzing and reconstructing the significant experiences of all of humanity.

This is not to say that everything that has happened everywhere and in all time periods can be recovered or is worth knowing, but that there is much to be gained by considering both the separate and interrelated stories of different societies and cultures. Making these connections is still another crucial ingredient of the "new" world history. It emphasizes connectedness and interactions of all kinds—cultural, economic, political, religious, and social—involving peoples, places, and processes. It makes comparisons and finds similarities. Emphasizing both the comparisons and interactions is critical to developing a global framework that can deepen and broaden historical understanding, whether the focus is on a specific country or region or on the whole world.

The rise of the new world history as a discipline comes at an opportune time. The interest in world history in schools and among the general public is vast. We travel to one another's nations, converse and work with people around the world, and are changed by global events. War and peace affect populations worldwide as do economic conditions and the state of our environment, communications, and health and medicine. The New Oxford World History presents local histories in a global context and gives an overview of world events seen through the eyes of ordinary people. This combination of the local and the global further defines the new world history. Understanding the workings of global and local conditions in the past gives us tools for examining our own world and for envisioning the interconnected future that is in the making.

Bonnie G. Smith
Anand Yang

Preface

Iran has been at the nexus of world history for the past three thousand years. Situated at the crossroads between East and West, Iran has been marked by its encounters with other civilizations and has influenced them with its own. Indeed, traces of Iranian culture can be seen throughout the world, from the very notion of Paradise (Avestan *pairi daeza*, "walled garden") to Persian carpets, which are a nearly universal marker of status and beauty. Iran—which Westerners called Persia until 1935—played a pivotal role in the early self-conceptualization of the West, projected as the essentialized "Other" by which ancient Greece defined itself.

Somewhat ironically, many of the major scholarly figures in medieval times who transmitted this same classical "Western" culture back to Europe were Iranians—although they are often mistakenly referred to as Arabs, since they usually wrote in Arabic, which was the scholarly language of the time. The pre-Islamic Iranian religion of Zoroastrianism provided many of the basic notions now found in Judaism, Christianity, and Islam.

Today, Iran is best known for its stubborn refusal to submit to Western hegemony; as a result, the country continues to be cast into the role of the Other, in opposition to which Westerners define and promote their own values. What Westerners often fail to appreciate, however, is that in the Asian sphere—where most of the world's population lives—Iran is often viewed in far more positive terms. Indeed, Iran is seen by many Asians as the very fountainhead of civilization, quite similar to how Westerners perceive ancient Greece and Rome. Persian literature, in particular, has deeply marked Turkey, Central Asia, and India; strong influences can be seen as well in areas such as architecture, administration, music, food, and religion. The Muslims of Asia, who represent three-quarters of all Muslims in the world, received Islam through a thickly Persian filter. A lesser-known fact is that the same is true for Asian Christianity, and even Chinese and Tibetan Buddhism.

When assessing the role of Iran in world history, therefore, it is important to recognize that the reach of Iranian civilization extends far beyond the borders of the present-day Islamic Republic—even beyond those of the earlier Iranian empires (Achaemenid, Parthian, Sasanian, Safavid), which were much larger. Still today, one should speak of not one but three Iranian states: apart from the Islamic Republic of Iran, Tajikistan and Afghanistan are both officially Persian-speaking and culturally Iranian. Uzbekistan has a large albeit mostly unrecognized Persian-speaking population, concentrated in the cities of Samarkand and Bukhara. The Kurds, who are spread out over half a dozen countries and constitute the fourth largest ethnic group in the Middle East, are also part of the larger Iranian group, as are the Baluch of Iran and Pakistan, the Pushtuns of Afghanistan and Pakistan, and the Ossetes and the Tats of the Caucasus.

Further afield, Iranian ideas and practices shaped those of cultures from the Balkans to India and China until quite recent times. The primary aim of the present work is to highlight the extraordinarily broad range of contributions Iranians have made to world history through the spread of their cultural norms, which were adopted in various forms by peoples from the Mediterranean to the Indian Ocean, and along the Silk Roads as far as China, from prehistoric times up to the present.

Iranians today are often pained by the mostly negative ways their culture is portrayed in Western media. Many prefer to distance themselves from the current government of Iran, which they do not see as properly representing who they are or the role they see as rightfully theirs in the world. At the same time, Iranians' pride in their own history remains unshaken and unassailable. But what exactly are the defining features of the "Iranian cultural identity" that is the source of this pride?

The Persian language (*farsi*) is of course a central component of this identity. Another is the "Land of Iran" (*Iran-zamin*), which extends well beyond the country's present-day borders. Yet another basic element is a shared cultural memory, most fully embodied in the tenth-century epic poem known as the *Book of Kings* (*Shah-nameh*), which is a legendary history of the Iranian people from the dawn of Creation up to the Arab conquest of the seventh century—an event that symbolically marks the "End of Civilization" on some level, even though it was the historical starting point for the Islamic identity most Iranians now share and with which Westerners tend to associate them. This paradox, about which more is said later, needs to be carefully considered by anyone wishing to better understand the Iranian psyche.

Language, land, and a shared memory seem to suffice for most discussions on cultural identity, but this simple framework masks a far more complicated underlying reality. In fact, cultural identities are almost always highly complex, and treating them as if they were clear and straightforward categories leads to all kinds of abuses. One need only consider the many "ethnic cleansing" campaigns that characterized the twentieth century to see the harm that can result from such oversimplifications.

In the case of Iran, certainly, each of these three "defining features" presents problems. The Persian language, while it has served as a marker of high culture throughout much of Asia for more than a thousand years, is actually the native language of only about half the population of modern Iran; at the same time, millions of native Persian-speakers live in other countries such as Afghanistan, Tajikistan, and Uzbekistan. Throughout the ancient period, three successive Iranian empires used Aramaic—a Semitic tongue—as the principal language of government; on the other hand, Persian was the administrative language of large parts of India for more than eight centuries, and the total corpus of Indo-Persian documents may exceed that of Iran proper.

The "Land of Iran" is, historically speaking, a highly fluid imaginary construct, spilling beyond borders—sometimes far beyond—which themselves were constantly shifting. The Sasanians (224–651 CE) had a clear enough conception of "the Realm of the Aryans" (*Eranshahr*) that they built permanent walls (still visible today) to mark the four corners of their empire. Yet even then, many Iranians lived outside the territory of *Eranshahr*, in Anatolia, Transoxiana, and China.

And as for the *Book of Kings* as a repository of cultural memory, it has been every bit as popular in Turkey, Central Asia, and India as it is in Iran. Adding to the irony, this tale of pre-Islamic Iranian heroes—which treats the coming of Islam as an apocalyptic tragedy—was composed by a Muslim poet (Abo'l-Qasem Ferdowsi), for a Muslim audience, and ultimately offered to a Turkish royal patron (Mahmud of Ghazna).

So much for "Iranian" culture—what of the "Iranian" people? Persian is a descendant of the Iranian branch of tongues which themselves are descended from Proto-Indo-European, the putative ancestor of English, French, German, Russian, Greek, Irish, Armenian, Hindi, and many other languages. (It has no genetic relation to Arabic or Turkish.) But merely speaking a language proves little about one's biological ancestry or group affiliation; all of history's most widespread idioms (Latin, Arabic, Spanish, English, Russian, Chinese) succeeded because they were adopted by peoples who originally spoke something else.

Speakers of proto-Iranian arrived in their present location only a little more than three thousand years ago. As newcomers to the region they were outnumbered, sometimes vastly, by the existing inhabitants who represented a wide range of languages and cultures. Some of them—the Elamites and Babylonians, for example, and perhaps "Jiroftians" as well—were heirs to great and ancient civilizations of their own. These peoples did not simply cease to exist, and while they may in many cases have adopted Iranian speech, their own cultural heritages were incorporated as elements of what came to be recognized as "Iranian" civilization in historical times. In fact, like most great civilizations, the Iranian should be understood as a *composite* culture made up of many diverse components. From ancient times to the present, Iranian society has been multiethnic, multilingual, and multireligious.

Even more important, this composite civilization we call "Iranian" always lived in dynamic interaction with its neighbors—Mesopotamian, Greek, Indian, and Chinese—and the influences were inevitably mutual. Thus, searching for "essential elements" by which it can be defined may be as elusive as looking for elementary particles in quantum physics. Taking a lesson from science, it may be more appropriate to consider Iranian civilization as a historically persistent pattern of appearances, which are nevertheless in constant flux.

CHAPTER 1

A Convergence of Land and Language (3500–550 BCE)

Darius the Great, who consolidated the Persian (Achaemenid) Empire during a thirty-six-year reign from 522 to 486 BCE, has left us history's first documented statement of explicitly Iranian self-identification. As he states in one of his royal inscriptions: "[I am] an Achaemenid, a Persian, son of a Persian, an Aryan, having Aryan lineage."[1] Following a framework still observed by many in the Middle East today, Darius identifies himself first in terms of family, then by tribe, and finally according to a broader category, what we might refer to today as "race" or "nation."

"Iran" derives from the same root as "Aryan": *heryos*, a word that, in a language spoken on the Eurasian steppes some five thousand years ago, meant "a member of our group." By perhaps fifteen centuries later, this self-designation had acquired the meaning "the noble ones" (that is to say, "us"). The people who used this word to describe themselves extended it to the place where they lived: *Airyanam Vaejo*, or "Land of the Noble Ones." However, since their history included centuries of southwestern migration from their original homeland near the Ural Mountains in Siberia, Airyanam Vaejo was not the same place from one period to the next. In other words, "Iran" was not always where it is now; it was farther north, then farther east.

In linguistics, "Iranian" is a subgroup within the Indo-European language family. All languages within the family are descended from a common ancestor language. For the sake of convenience, we situate the speakers of this language somewhere north of the Black and Caspian Seas during the fourth millennium BCE. But this period is merely a snapshot in time: the people in question had earlier come from somewhere else, and later moved on, while their language was constantly changing as languages do. From time to time bands split off from the main tribe and went their separate ways, and as these separations became permanent, their respective dialects diverged into distinct languages. Speakers of the branches that evolved into Celtic, Germanic, Italic, and Greek headed west into Europe; others, including Indo-Iranian- and Tokharian-speakers, went in the opposite direction. (The ancestors of the Slavs seem to have more or less stayed put.)

This common linguistic ancestor is helpful for reconstructing the prehistory of Iranians and other Indo-European peoples. A comparison of their various myths and material cultures can tell us something about the Indo-Europeans' ancestors themselves—how they lived, how they viewed things, what they invented, and the impact they had on the world. The "Aryans," as they called themselves, also influenced non-Indo-European cultures all across northern Eurasia, from Eastern Europe to Mongolia and beyond. Their myths and rituals even influenced those of prehistoric China and Japan.[2]

The Aryan culture preserved in our fourth millennium BCE snapshot was distinctive in a number of respects. Its people survived largely by herding domesticated animals, shifting between summer and winter pastures—a form of social economy anthropologists refer to as "pastoral-nomadic." They measured wealth in terms of ownership of cattle and sheep, which they often acquired by raiding their neighbors' livestock. They were highly patriarchal and recognized clear social divisions between three classes: priests/rulers, warriors, and herders and craftsmen. (These social divisions laid the basis for what would later become the caste system in India.) The pastoral-nomadic culture of the steppe-dwellers has been surprisingly resistant over the past five millennia, surviving in its essentials well into the twentieth century when as much as one-third of the population of the greater Iranian world still continued to follow this way of life.

Warrior ethics have always been prominent in nomadic societies. To ancient Aryan raiders, cattle, land, and women were not so much "stolen" as "liberated" from inferior peoples who didn't deserve them. Their poets celebrated these values in heroic tales, some of which made their way into written texts such as the Sanskrit *Rig Veda*, the Zoroastrian *Avesta*, and the Persian *Book of Kings*.

The myth of the hero who slays the dragon—often rescuing an imprisoned maiden in the process—is found in so many Indo-European cultures that it must date back to the early common period. The Avestan hymn to Anahita contains one such episode, where the hero Thraetaona asks the goddess for the strength to "overcome the Giant Dragon with three mouths, three heads, six eyes, a thousand tricks. . . . May I also carry off his two beloved women Sanghawaci and Arnawaci, who have the most beautiful, the most wonderful bodies to be won in the world of the living!"[3]

By around 3500 BCE our steppe nomads had domesticated the horse, enabling them to become the most mobile people on the planet. Some fifteen centuries later they developed the war chariot, which gave them a decisive advantage over their enemies in battle. It is perhaps no historical accident that the descendants of these warlike people went on to conquer most of the world, as attested by the fact that Indo-European is the most widespread of all the language families.

Climate surely spurred Indo-European speakers to fan out through centuries of successive migrations. The Eurasian steppe is a place of extremes: long, cold winters and hot, dry summers. According to Iranian mythology, the original Airyanam Vaejo had ten months of winter (created by the Evil Spirit) and two months of summer. Hell, rather than possessing eternal fires, is described as a place of intense cold: "Regarding the cold, dry, stony, and dark interior of mysterious hell . . . the darkness is fit to grasp with the hand, and the stench is fit to cut with a knife."[4]

This origin myth fits neatly with archaeological evidence from sites around the southern Ural Mountains, on the western fringes of Siberia. Typical of these sites is Sintashta, which was a fortified town during the centuries before and after 2000 BCE where burial techniques correspond very closely to those described in the Sanskrit *Veda*s held sacred by today's Hindus in India. These burials contain the results of ritual horse sacrifices (Sanskrit *asvamedha*), as well as the earliest remains yet discovered of spoke-wheeled chariots.[5]

The oldest text in the Sanskrit language, the *Rig Veda*, was first written down in India around the seventh century BCE, but it preserves an oral tradition going back, apparently . . . to the southern Ural Mountains, during the centuries before and after 2000 BCE. The people associated with the Sintashta site probably spoke a proto-Indo-Iranian language that was the common ancestor to both the Iranian and Indic linguistic branches, including Avestan and Sanskrit. Having access to copper mines in the Urals, the Sintashta people smelted bronze, which they traded with people in places as far away as Central Asia and even Mesopotamia.

Over the following millennium their descendants migrated southward, leaving burial mounds, pottery, and other traces throughout northern Central Asia. Known to archaeologists as the Andronovo peoples, some of these migrants may have introduced the wheeled chariots and advanced metallurgy that appear for the first time in China around 1200 BCE. Others continued their migrations to the southeast, over the Hindu Kush Mountains and into South Asia. The main body of proto-Iranians, meanwhile, moved more slowly but directly south, to the east of the Caspian Sea, eventually making their way into the arid, mountainous plateau region that now bears their name.

What would come to be the Iranian heartland in historic times was already inhabited by a wide range of peoples, including settled agricultural societies that predated the arrival of Iranian-speakers on the plateau by almost seven thousand years. The foundations of permanent dwellings, milling implements, and storage vessels for grain found in the central Zagros Mountains of western Iran all point to the transition from hunting and gathering to agricultural societies around the early eighth millennium BCE. Goats were probably first domesticated here, and sheep, cattle, and pigs were also present. Wheat and barley were indigenous to the region. Contemporary Neolithic sites have been identified in northeastern Iran as well, demonstrating that all parts of the plateau had known human habitation prior to the arrival of the Iranians.

Since the pre-existing inhabitants of what would become Iran were absorbed into Iranian culture over time, these older societies must be reconstructed by means of the archaeological record they left behind. Whenever Iranian-speaking groups settled in new areas, they would have mixed with the native population and the resulting cultural influences would have been mutual, although the Iranian language eventually prevailed.

The first major civilization that the southward-moving proto-Iranians encountered was a Bronze Age culture stretching eastward from the Caspian Sea, between the mountainous region of modern Afghanistan and the parched steppes of present-day Turkmenistan and Uzbekistan. This civilization, which flourished from the late third to early second millennium BCE, left behind a material culture of walled towns, ceramics, tools, and jewelry that was uncovered by Soviet excavations during the twentieth century. The Soviets labeled the ensemble of related sites after the ancient Greek names for the corresponding two provinces of the Persian Empire—Bactria (the northern part of what is now Afghanistan) and Margiana (roughly modern Turkmenistan)—calling it the Bactria-Margiana Archaeological Complex, or BMAC.

Unlike the Iranians, the BMAC peoples were settled agriculturalists, cultivating wheat and barley. This sustenance they supplemented with animal husbandry; a recent BMAC excavation in North Khorasan province unearthed the remains of a smelly dish called *kaleh-pacheh*—the "head and feet [of sheep]"—which is still enjoyed in Iran today as a breakfast delicacy and a humorous means of horrifying foreign guests.

Farming in this arid region depended on a sophisticated system of irrigation canals, called *qanat*s in modern Persian, which brought runoff snowmelt from nearby mountains via underground channels. The BMAC people traded widely: with the Elamites to the southwest, the Indus Valley peoples to the southeast, and the Sintashta/Andronovo culture (that is, the Indo-Iranians) to the north. The trans-Asian trade network we call the Silk Road had probably already begun to emerge by this time, and the BMAC peoples were situated directly in the heart of it. While the Silk Road is commonly said to have been "opened" during the first century BCE, in fact these paths, beaten down by centuries of human traffic across Eurasia, are to a large extent dictated by geography and probably date far back into prehistoric times.

Since the BMAC peoples left no written records, their language is unknown, although it contributed a number of loanwords to Indo-Iranian. These include—tellingly, since loanwords typically indicate cultural borrowings—the words for "camel," "donkey," and "wheat." The migrating Indo-Iranians mixed with the BMAC throughout the second millennium BCE and gradually formed a hybrid society. This process of cultural synthesis can be considered the first major step in the "civilizing" of the warlike Iranian-speaking tribes.

The pattern is repeated endlessly throughout the history of Eurasia, with steppe nomads and oasis settlers all the way from Europe to China maintaining an uneasy relationship that alternated between raiding and trading. When the nomads did choose to settle, they would quickly assimilate into the urban culture, although they often succeeded in imposing their language, as Iranian-speakers did in ancient times. The nomad-settler dynamic remained an essential feature of Iranian society up to the early twentieth century.

As Iranian tribes continued their movements south and west onto the plateau they came into contact with a number of other settled societies, some of which had long been established in southeastern Iran, southern Mesopotamia, and eastern Anatolia. In southeastern Iran, excavations south of the town of Jiroft have uncovered relics of a culture dating back at least to the third millennium BCE and possibly earlier. Discussions about how to interpret these finds have been controversial, and scholars dispute whether all the artifacts associated with Jiroft really came from there. Because these discoveries are so recent (beginning in 2001) and have been the province almost entirely of Iranian archaeologists, it is too early to assess the impact of the claims made about them, but the possibilities are very intriguing.

The Jiroft excavations have uncovered some impressive building structures. These include a massive ziggurat (a terraced step pyramid), more than twelve hundred feet square, as well as a two-story citadel and a fourteen-room house. The ziggurat has been claimed to date to around 2300 BCE, which would make it older than any of those existing in Mesopotamia. A number of inscriptions have also been found. They are in an unknown script, but Iranian archaeologists have asserted that they are older than the earliest writings in Sumerian, the language of the Sumer people who inhabited southern Mesopotamia during the third millennium BCE. If true, this could mean that writing—long assumed to have been an invention of the Sumerians—was first devised by the Jiroft culture and then spread to Mesopotamia from there.

To the east of Jiroft, on the border of Afghanistan, lie the remains of Shahr-e sukhteh, "the Burnt City," a large Bronze Age town that flourished between 3200 and 2100 BCE. Its culture appears to be related to that of the Jiroft site, leading some (mainly Iranian) archaeologists to suggest that we are on the verge of piecing together the existence of a major, hitherto unknown ancient civilization situated between those of Mesopotamia and the Indus Valley.

The Burnt City site has revealed a number of "firsts," including the oldest known artificial eye, the oldest backgammon set and dice, and damaged skulls showing that the inhabitants practiced brain surgery and dentistry (how successfully is unclear). A goblet was found which, when spun, shows a deer leaping in motion—perhaps the world's earliest example of animation.

An animated vase, made in eastern Iran in the late third millennium BCE, is possibly the world's earliest example of animation: when it is spun, the gazelle appears to leap; this illustration demonstrates that effect. Found at Shahr-e sukhteh, the vase may be connected with the little-understood Jiroft culture that existed between Mesopotamia to the west and the Indus Valley to the east. Reproduction by Michał Sałaban, courtesy Wikimedia Commons

At its opposite western edge, marked by the Zagros mountain chain, the Iranian plateau spills out onto the fertile plains watered by the Tigris and Euphrates rivers—Mesopotamia, "the land between the rivers." Although this region is associated today with the modern nation of Iraq, from twenty-five hundred years ago until early modern times it was politically part of Iran. Indeed, because its population and economy were considerably greater than that of the Iranian plateau, throughout much of history Mesopotamia was the political and economic center of the Iranian world, although a majority of its inhabitants were neither ethnically nor linguistically Iranian.

The ancient language of neighboring Elam, for instance, has no confirmed links to any other. Originally based in the highlands of the southern Zagros Mountains, around 4000 BCE the Elamites founded a capital and economic center called Shushan on the alluvial plains to the south of the mountain chain. A number of ethnic and linguistic groups inhabited this area, but from the early fifth to the early first millennium BCE Elamite culture dominated and spread in all directions. To the northeast, a ziggurat at Tepe Sialk in central Iran (near the city of Kashan), dated to around 2900 BCE, is thought to have been built by the Elamites.

The alluvial plains are dry and very hot for much of the year, so Elamite agriculture depended on irrigation channeled off from the mighty Karun River. Due to the region's climatic extremes, seasonal migration between the mountains and lowlands was the norm for many of it inhabitants, including a succession of royal dynasties who had both summer and winter capitals. The Zagros uplands have a mixed economy of sheep and goat herding and agriculture going back almost ten thousand years.

In addition to Shushan, by the late third millennium the Elamites had established a highland capital at Anshan, west of the modern city of Shiraz. An Elamite ruler was thus often referred to as "the King of Shushan and Anshan." Subjected to invasions from Mesopotamia throughout the second and early first millennium BCE, Anshan fell into decay. Eventually, during the mid- to late seventh century BCE, the region fell under the control of an Iranian tribe known in Assyrian records as the Parsumash who had moved south from the central Zagros Mountains under pressure from a related Iranian tribe, the Medes. They eventually gave their name to this region—Parsa—which the Greeks called "Persis" (Persia) and is now the Iranian province of Fars.

Mesopotamian states depended on the mountainous lands to the east to supply them with such essential materials as wood, metals, and stone; sometimes these were traded and sometimes taken by force. Cuneiform records from the third millennium BCE onward document repeated Mesopotamian attempts to bring the Elamite lands under control. Given its position on the southern plain, Shushan was more subject to political and cultural influence from Babylonia in the central Mesopotamian lowlands than was the less-accessible mountain region of Anshan. This influence can be seen notably in the realm of religion: at Shushan, Babylonian as well as Elamite deities were worshipped. Written records from Shushan—mostly lists of kings and conquests—are predominantly in Sumerian and, later, Akkadian (a north Semitic language). In Anshan, on the other hand, Elamite was the more prevalent language. The material culture of Shushan, such as pottery, shows Mesopotamian influences in its techniques and decorative designs.

The polytheistic Elamite religion differed from one location to another. A ziggurat constructed just east of Shushan around 1250 BCE contained temples to both highland and lowland deities and may have represented an attempt to unify the two regions. The Elamites gave special prominence to goddesses, a fact taken by some scholars as indicating that their society was originally matriarchal. The goddess Kiririsha, identified in the northern part of Elam as Pinikir, was the primary female deity, second only to her husband, Humban. Many of her features, such as ensuring fertility and health, appear to have been later assimilated into those of the Iranian water goddess, Anahita, whose cult came to flourish in the same region from the Achaemenid period onward.

Mesopotamia's influence over Sushan waned as the Gutians, a nomadic mountain people (or peoples) from the central Zagros range, raided and eventually conquered much of Mesopotamia during the late third millennium BCE. In fact, it seems that the Mesopotamian records use "Gutian" as a catch-all term for raiders from the eastern mountains, so it probably did not refer to a single people. None of the sources has anything good to say about the Gutians; they are seen as hostile savages who kidnap women and children and don't respect proper religious rites. One Sumerian text describes them as having "human face, dog's cunning, and monkey's build."[6]

During the second half of the second millennium BCE, the Kassites of the southern Zagros Mountains introduced the domesticated horse into Mesopotamian culture. Not surprisingly, given the significant

The ziggurat at Chogha Zanbil, near the modern city of Shush in Khuzestan province, southwestern Iran, was constructed around 1250 BCE by the Elamite king Untash-Napirisha. The complex contained temples to twelve separate deities and has been seen as an attempt to meld the religions of the highland and lowland cultures of Elam. It is theorized that ziggurats were built in imitation of mountains, especially where previously mountain-dwelling peoples had migrated to lowland areas. Arian Zwegers/Wikimedia Commons/CC-BY-2.0

military advantage this represented, the Kassites worshipped horses as divine creatures. The introduction of cavalry permanently altered the nature of warfare throughout the region, and a ready supply of horses became indispensable to any large-scale military conquest.

Further north in the Zagros region, in the lands to the west of Lake Urmia, Hurrians and Armenians were both well represented within the multiethnic state of Urartu, known in the Hebrew Bible as the Kingdom of Ararat. Urartian civilization left many traces, especially its monumental architecture, dam building, and the practice of carving inscriptions onto rock cliffs, all of which the Iranian Medes and Persians adopted several centuries later. Like the Kassites, the Medes were horse breeders, which made them both an economic necessity to the Assyrians (who were the major imperial power in the region during the ninth to seventh centuries BCE) and a constant threat to them as well.

At some point during the proto-Iranians' southward migrations, perhaps toward the end of the second millennium BCE, a hereditary priest from one of their clans began to compose ritual hymns of a very distinctive nature. The priest's name was Zarathushtra, better known in the West as Zoroaster.[7] His hymns, called the *Gatha*s (songs), dramatically reconfigured the relationships and rituals associated with the old Indo-Iranian pantheon, elevating one deity, Mazda (the Lord of Wisdom), to the status of Supreme Being, while relegating the others to the level of either Mazda's servants (*ahura*s) or his demonic enemies (*daeva*s).

The Gathas present the world as a battleground between the forces of good (*asha*, "cosmic order") and evil (*druj*, "the Lie"). All good things come from Ahura Mazda, whereas evil is due entirely to the workings of a dark spirit, Angra Mainyu; it is up to each person to choose a side. Zoroaster complains bitterly in the Gathas about the warrior ethics that ruled his pastoral society, assigning cattle thieves and their patron deities to the legions of the wicked: "Those who by their evil guiding wisdom and by the utterances of their tongues will only increase Wrath and Obstruction, they who tend no cattle among those who do and not one of whom has overcome bad deeds by good deeds, they will define the old gods as the vision-soul of the one possessed by the Lie."[8]

The exact time and place Zoroaster lived remain open to speculation, but on linguistic and sociological grounds it would seem appropriate to place him somewhere in southern Central Asia shortly after the Indo-Iranian split during the second millennium BCE. The language of the Gathas, called Old Avestan, is an east Iranian dialect very close to the Sanskrit of the Vedas. Both texts were transmitted orally for many centuries, until each was finally written down—the former in Iran and the latter in India—by priests who no longer fully understood either language.

The Avesta, which became the sacred text of Zoroastrianism, includes the Gathas, plus a ritual manual called the Seven-Part Sacrifice, as well as other texts in a related dialect called Younger Avestan. The latter are mostly sacrificial liturgies devoted to deities other than Mazda, including the warrior god Mithra and the water goddess Anahita. As in Vedic and numerous other ancient religions, the veneration of fire was central to the Mazda cult, to the extent that Zoroastrians were often inaccurately described as "fire worshippers." It is likely that for at least thirteen centuries or more, Zoroaster's radical religious vision was preserved by a particular priestly school—perhaps among the tribes known as the Medes—and not necessarily by Iranians as a whole. During this time, many if not most Iranian groups continued to follow their own local variations of sacrificial polytheistic religion.

By the late second millennium BCE, Iranian-speaking tribes had begun to move into the region that would come to be known as Iran, beginning east of the Caspian Sea and spreading westward along the southern flank of the Alborz Mountains. The various Iranian tribes had many things in common, and they spoke closely related dialects, but there were significant differences among them. The Medes and the Persians, who settled in the central and western parts of the plateau during the early first millennium BCE, gradually integrated themselves into the existing social economy of ancient West Asia, eventually becoming significant new players in the imperial dynamics of the region.

The Sakas, on the other hand, maintained most of their warrior-nomadic ways, continuing to occupy the steppe regions to the east, north, and west of the Caspian Sea. They frequently raided the settled populations of the Iranian plateau and sometimes overran them entirely. Farther west, their incursions into the territories north of the Black Sea brought them into contact with Greek colonies—the Greeks referred to them as Scythians or "mounted archers." ("Scythian" comes from the Indo-European root *skud*, which has an English cognate, "to shoot.") With their high-speed battle techniques, the Sakas were the masters of the steppe for many centuries, leaving their mark through incursions as far afield as Eastern Europe, China, and India.

Saka culture is known for its art production, including brilliant 22-karat gold jewelry, which usually featured animal figures and came to characterize what contemporary art historians refer to as "steppe art." From the seventh century BCE to the second century CE substantial numbers of Saka nomads adopted settled life and began to trade, especially with the Greeks of the Pontic Steppe region north of the Black Sea. The art from this period of both the Greeks and the Sakas shows mutual influences stemming from the encounter between their respective cultures, refined urban in the case of the Greeks and rustic nomadic in the case of the Sakas. Saka art often featured horses—perhaps the most central element of their culture—and also fantastic depictions of the Goddess, sometimes shown with snakes for limbs, who was apparently the main focus of their religion. The Sakas also appear to have invented the hand-knotted carpet; the oldest surviving example of this technique was found at Pazyryk in the Altai Mountains on the border between Kazakhstan and Mongolia, and dates to the fifth century BCE. For nomads living in tents, carpets were the most essential item of furniture, and the same is true in many traditional Iranian homes today.

Saka tribes based in southeastern Iran began to invade the northwestern part of the Indian subcontinent beginning in the mid-second century BCE. During the next few centuries they remained an active though numerically small component of north Indian society, on several occasions managing to establish culturally mixed kingdoms. Northwest India at that time was highly cosmopolitan, a meeting ground of Indian, Iranian, Greek, and Tokharian cultures and an important center of early Buddhism. The cultural mix characterizing the Gandhara civilization, which flourished under the Kushan dynasty (first to third centuries CE), can be seen in the representation of the Buddha and Buddhist tales through art using Hellenistic forms. Kushan coins illustrate this cosmopolitanism as well, incorporating languages and religious symbols from the full range of peoples inhabiting the empire.

The eastern Sakas, who eventually settled in the city of Khotan (now in Xinjiang province of western China), adopted Buddhism and became notable for their literary production, which was primarily Buddhist texts—these date mainly from the fourth to tenth centuries CE. The Saka legacy in Khotan shows the central importance of Iranians in the eastward spread of Buddhism.

The earliest written reference to an Iranian tribe, the Medes, appears in official records of the Assyrian Empire dating to 881 BCE. The Assyrians counted the Mede lands, or Madaya—a province situated south of the Alborz Mountains and east of the Zagros—as one of their vassal states for the next two centuries. (Territories just to the south, controlled by a closely related Iranian tribe, the Parsa [Persians], held a similar status beginning in 744 BCE.) The major economic activity of the Medes was horse breeding, and they were the main providers of horses for the Assyrian army.

The Assyrians had a policy of deporting the populations of conquered territories, and during their overlordship they transplanted many Medes and Persians into Syria. Likewise, following their conquest of the Kingdom of Israel in 722 BCE, the Assyrians deported many Israelites to Iranian lands to the east: this migration was the beginning of the historical Jewish diaspora. While the Assyrians' policy had no other object than their own political control, it had the unintended benefit of bringing diverse cultures into contact and fostering mutual influences.

The encounter between Iranians and Israelites would prove to be one of the most significant in the history of religions. Avestan notions that came to be central to later religions such as Christianity and Islam—including the existence of heaven and hell, angels and demons, the Devil, the Resurrection of the dead and the Last Judgment, and the restoration of the divine kingdom by a Savior figure following an apocalyptic battle between the forces of good and evil—are all absent from the Israelites' sacrifice-based Yahweh cult prior to their contact with Iranians. The Israelites would therefore seem to have absorbed these ideas from Zoroastrianism, which was probably brought from Central Asia to western Iran by a priestly class of the Medes known as the Magi. The biblical book of II Kings specifically notes that following the Assyrian conquest, Israelites were deported to "Halah and Habor by the River Gozan and in the cities of the Medes,"[9] which means that they were settled among Iranians in precisely the area where the Zoroastrian rite is likely to have been most prevalent.

In a rock relief at the burial site of a Median ruler—possibly Cyaxares I (who may be the figure to the left)—the ruler faces a Mazdaean priest before a fire altar, in what is possibly the earliest known depiction of Zoroastrian ritual. A rare example of Median architecture, this mausoleum shows an emerging style combining Greek-style pillars, Assyrian iconography, and the Urartian model of building funerary monuments in honor of important individuals. Photo by author

According to the Greek historian Herodotus, during the eighth and seventh centuries BCE, six Mede tribes formed an alliance and began to rebel against their Assyrian overlords. In about 672 BCE they managed to expel the Assyrians altogether and assert their independence, forming, in Herodotus's words, a "Median empire" (*medikos logos*).[10] In 612, the Medes went on to conquer the Assyrian capital at Nineveh in northern Mesopotamia, which allowed them to extend their power into Anatolia. Contemporary scholars, citing the lack of archaeological evidence such as imperial infrastructures, have questioned whether in fact the Medes ever established a unified state, so calling it an "empire" may be a bit of an exaggeration. In fact, little is known about Median politics after the Medes expelled the Assyrians, up to 550 BCE when they were conquered by their southern relatives, the Persians.

CHAPTER 2

Iran and the Greeks (550–247 BCE)

One of the key moments in Jewish history as described in the Hebrew Bible is the conquest of Babylon by the Persian king Cyrus in 539 BCE. The Book of Isaiah refers to Cyrus as "God's anointed" (literally, a Messiah), and portrays the Persians as instruments of the Hebrew god, Yahweh, sent to liberate the Israelites from their Babylonian captivity: "I will raise up Cyrus in my righteousness: I will make all his ways straight. He will rebuild my city and set my exiles free, but not for a price or reward, says Yahweh Almighty."[1]

Cyrus the Great, as he is known in the West, was actually Kurash II, the King of Anshan in Elam. It was under his leadership that the Parsa tribe—who by that point were becoming an ethnic mix of Iranians and Elamites—successfully rebelled against their Median overlords in 550 BCE, reversing their prior relationship and turning the Medes into Persian vassals.

In fact, Babylon was home to many captive peoples, and Cyrus liberated all of them. He accorded citizenship to everyone, along with the freedom to live wherever they wished within the boundaries of his now vast empire. Ironically, few Israelites actually took advantage of this opportunity to return to Palestine, which had been laid waste by the Babylonian invasions several decades earlier. On the contrary, many stayed on as free citizens in Persian-ruled Babylonia. This region would become the center of Jewish civilization for the next thousand years or more, eventually producing the Talmudic religion that came to represent its essence.

Other groups of Israelites preferred to move even farther east, settling throughout the lands of the plateau where they became integrated into Iranian society. (The biblical books of Esther and Daniel are both set in Iran.) The Jewish tradition developed to a large extent within an Iranian cultural environment and was shaped by it in many ways.

The Bible exaggerates, however, in according the Israelites a central place of importance for the Persians. Cyrus was first and foremost a strategist, and he sought to build support among all the various nations under his rule (among whom the Israelites were hardly the most numerous or significant) by respecting their individual norms and traditions. On entering Babylon he paid homage to the Babylonian supreme deity, Marduk, and had a written proclamation of his policies engraved on a cylinder that was then buried within the foundations of Marduk's temple. This cylinder—which may in fact have been one of many—was rediscovered by archaeologists during the nineteenth century and has since become one of the most discussed documents of the ancient world.

The "Cyrus cylinder," as it is often called, is actually a rather small object, measuring less than nine inches across. Its text, which is in Akkadian cuneiform script, is divided into six sections, each praising various aspects of Cyrus's enlightened deeds since entering Babylon. The first section—belying the claims of the Bible that Cyrus was acting on behalf of the Hebrew god—associates Cyrus with Marduk and implies that he came to Babylon to restore proper rule in Marduk's city: "[Marduk] inspected and checked all the countries, seeking the upright king of his choice. He took the hand of Cyrus, King of the city of Anshan, and called him by his name, proclaiming him aloud for the kingship over all of everything."[2] The remainder of the text continues to refer to Marduk and other Babylonian gods; neither the Hebrew god nor any Iranian deities are mentioned. Clearly the text is intended for a Babylonian audience, portraying Cyrus as a legitimate ruler in the established Mesopotamian tradition.

In modern times the Cyrus cylinder has often been claimed as the "world's first document on human rights." Indeed, a replica of it adorns the entrance lobby to the United Nations building in New York, and it has been cherished by Iranians as a national symbol since the early 1970s. Interpreting the cylinder as a human rights manifesto is anachronistic, however, and modern-day nationalist Iranian claims to it are overstretched. Cyrus's conciliatory policy toward his subjects was a departure from the prior abuses of the Babylonians and the Assyrians, but it was based mainly on the pragmatic needs of running a multinational state.

While the Persian Empire was the direct heir to Elamite civilization, its perpetuation of Median traditions is more immediately visible. The Persians adopted Median titles (e.g., "satrap" for "governor") and their system of administration, and they used the Median capital Ecbatana (modern Hamedan) as their summer residence. The

The "Cyrus cylinder" bears a cuneiform inscription of the policies of the Persian Emperor Cyrus the Great following his conquest of Babylon in 539 BCE. Claimed today to be the world's first declaration of human rights, a replica of the cylinder is on display in the entrance hall to the United Nations building in New York City. Replica from the collection of the Centre for Iranian Studies, Concordia University.

monumental architecture of the Persians followed that of the Medes (and the Urartians before them), for example, in their use of colonnaded reception halls and rock-cliff royal inscriptions.

Having subjugated the Median lands, Cyrus launched an attack against the Lydians in central Anatolia. This step in his expansionist campaign was ostensibly taken in defense of a Median possession that had been seized by the Lydian ruler Croesus, who despite his loss to the Persians, came to be immortalized in Western tradition as a symbol of massive wealth (as in the expression, "richer than Croesus"). The Lydian king may have been the first ruler in history to mint gold coins, which were then adopted by the victorious Persians as their principal currency. Cyrus brought Lydian and Ionian architects and stonemasons back to Iran and set them to work constructing his new capital at Pasargadae, where Greek building styles are evident.

Cyrus met his death in 530 BCE, fighting against one of the nomadic Saka tribes of Central Asia, the Massagatae. By that time he had carved out the largest empire the world had yet known, stretching from the

Eastern Mediterranean to the marches of the northwestern Indian subcontinent. Under his son, Cambyses (Pers. Kambujieh) II, Egypt as well was brought under Persian rule.

The imperial administration under Cyrus, like that of the Medes, was based on the indirect rule of the provinces through satraps (governors) appointed personally by him. Rebellions from regional power bases—that is, ambitious local satraps in league with tax-resistant landowners and their private armies conscripted from peasants and nomads—always had the potential to challenge the imperial government. Nevertheless, in its essence, this administrative model remained in place throughout successive empires ruling Iran, both native and foreign, for more than two millennia, well into the Islamic period.

Whereas Cyrus's proclamations portray him in the tradition of Elamite and Babylonian rulers, Darius (Darayavaush) I was the first imperial monarch to assert a distinctly Persian identity, and his inscriptions are the first written records of the Persian language. Beginning his career as a humble cavalryman in the army of Cambyses II, Darius assumed the throne in 522 BCE after a confusing political scrum during which either the emperor's brother or an imposter claiming to be him briefly seized power and Cambyses himself either committed suicide, died in an accident, or was assassinated.

Doubts regarding Darius's legitimacy sparked revolts in the provinces, and he spent the first part of his reign suppressing these. Once he had established control over the imperial heartlands, he turned his attention to Egypt and then to the Indus Valley, consolidating Persian rule in both regions. He also invaded Saka territory to the north, ostensibly to avenge the killing of Cyrus. From there he proceeded westward to Thrace, bringing many Greek-inhabited lands under Persian control. An alliance of Greek city-states finally halted the Persian advance into Greece at the Battle of Marathon in 490 BCE. (The original "marathon" was run by a courier who brought the news of Greek victory to Athens, twenty-six miles away.)

Darius not only succeeded in expanding and systematizing the Persian Empire; he also reformed it from within, ensuring the empire's lasting stability. The Greek philosopher Plato attributed the strength of the Persian Empire to the effectiveness of Darius's laws: "For by the laws he framed he has preserved the empire of the Persians even until this day."[3] The Old Persian word for law, *data*, was borrowed into the Semitic languages, including Aramaic and Hebrew, suggesting that the Persian model for prescribing social order was seen as innovative in the context of the ancient world.

Since the time of Cyrus, the empire had been a loose confederation of diverse states, each of which operated according to its own administrative norms. Darius reworked the provincial system into twenty satrapies, formalizing the fiscal responsibilities of each. He helped to standardize trade by introducing royal coinage in fixed weights of gold (the daric) and silver (the shekel)—these were the first coins in history to bear images of a person's face (his). He allocated substantial funds toward the construction of underground canals (*qanat*s), which facilitated the development of agriculture in Iran's dry climate.

Darius established Aramaic, not Persian, as the language of administration. This was likely because of the numerical and economic importance of the Semitic Mesopotamian population under his rule, but in his royal inscriptions he addressed a broader audience by using Persian and Elamite as well. He was consciously proud of the cosmopolitan nature of his empire, which his official proclamations describe as including "all nations and languages." (In practice he identified thirty.) The total population of the empire at the time was probably around fifty million, including both Iranian and non-Iranian citizens: aristocrats, landowners and peasants, merchants and craftsmen, nomads and slaves.

Darius referred to himself as "King of Kings," reflecting his multinational imperial vision. It was Darius who gave the empire its distinctive and lasting character, and his inscriptions are the first written sources to use the dynastic name "Achaemenid." (Cyrus the Great is often referred to as the founder of the Persian Empire, but there is some doubt about his exact relationship to the Achaemenid family line.) The Achaemenids had four capital cities, incorporating the political traditions of the major states they had absorbed: the former Elamite center of Shushan (henceforth known as Susa), Babylon in Mesopotamia, the Median capital of Ecbatana, and Persepolis, which they built themselves as a ceremonial site for celebrating the New Year every spring. These and provincial capitals from Anatolia and Egypt to Central Asia were linked by a system of royal roads, facilitating not only the movement of troops but also commerce, as well as mail—it was the Persians who developed the world's first postal system.

Despite the empire's proudly multinational character, the Achaemenids made a conscious distinction between Iranian peoples (*Arya*, including Persians, Medes, and Bactrians) and non-Iranians (*Anarya*) who were the majority. Non-Iranians paid higher taxes, while Iranians were better represented in the army. Darius's royal inscriptions also give the first clear indication that the Mazdaean religion of Zoroaster had achieved the level of royal patronage: "A great god is

Auramazda (Ahura Mazda), who created yonder heaven, who created this earth, who created man, who created happiness for man, who made Darius king, who bestowed on Darius this land, large, with good horses, with good men."[4]

Darius considered Ahura Mazda to be his personal patron deity, just as Cyrus had earlier adopted Marduk as his. But that did not make the Achaemenid state officially Zoroastrian. The Median Magi, custodians of the Zoroastrian rite, had apparently worked their way into Darius's inner circle, but it would be another eight centuries before they could exercise full religious authority over Iranian society. Within the general population, religious diversity was the norm among Iranians and non-Iranians alike. This consisted of a wide range of cults to local deities, as evidenced by the records of priestly commissions preserved in the so-called Persepolis fortification tablets. These documents mention only a tiny handful of ceremonies performed for Ahura Mazda, compared to much larger numbers dedicated to Elamite and other gods and goddesses.

In 515 BCE Darius began building the palace complex of Persepolis (from the Greek, *persis-polis*, "Parsa-the-city") just north of the modern city of Shiraz, and construction continued for about a hundred years thereafter. Persepolis was the Persians' springtime capital, a special ceremonial center used on the occasion of the Persian New Year, *Noruz*, when nobles from all across the realm brought tribute such as live animals or other valuables to the emperor. Processions of dozens of these gift-givers, each in their native garb, are depicted in stone engravings which are still preserved at the site.

Occurring exactly at the moment of the vernal equinox, Noruz was originally an agricultural festival symbolizing the ending of winter and the regeneration of life. Iranians seem to have adopted it from Mesopotamia, where its roots can be seen in the myth of the goddess Ishtar and her son/lover Tammuzi, who is sacrificed each autumn and enters the underworld, mourned by Ishtar with tearful laments until he returns to life in the spring. (This resurrection myth later served as the precedent for yet another springtime celebration, the Christian Easter.)

Mesopotamian traditions heavily influenced the monumental art of the Achaemenids as well. The *fravahr*—a winged disk with a human figure in the center—was used as a royal emblem from Darius's time onward. Originally derived from an Assyrian model representing the Semitic solar deity Ashur, the *fravahr* symbol was used in Achaemenid times to depict Ahura Mazda.

Subjects bring tribute to the Persian emperor in Persepolis. One of the four Achaemenid capitals, Persepolis was the site of the annual Persian New Year ceremonies every spring, when representatives from every province of the empire brought gifts for the king. The site was destroyed by Alexander the Great in 330 BCE. Persepolis, Fars province, southwestern Iran, photo by author.

For centuries to come, large numbers of Greeks and other ethnic groups would spend long periods as Persian subjects, especially in Anatolia and Mesopotamia, fostering considerable interaction and mutual influence between the two civilizations. Although the Greeks had managed to halt Darius's expansion at the Battle of Marathon, Persian and Greek armies continued to push the border back and forth for the next thousand years. Many Greeks attained important positions in Persian society, and even at Athens pro-Persian groups were present. Herodotus and other Greek writers popularized an "us-and-them" antagonism with their anti-Persian political propaganda, but on the ground Persians and Greeks often thrived together.

The history of the Achaemenid period is generally told in a way that emphasizes more or less constant battles between the two major powers of the Eastern Mediterranean, the Greeks and the Persians. Darius's successor, Xerxes (Khshayarsha) I, renewed the campaign against Greece and entered Athens, where he burned the Parthenon in 480 BCE. Two centuries later, Alexander of Macedon burned down Persepolis in revenge. What is often glossed over in discussions of the

A modern fravahr *(the most recognizable symbol in Zoroastrian religious iconography) is displayed above the entryway to a Zoroastrian fire temple in Mumbai, India. In ancient times the figure within the winged disk, borrowed from Assyrian art, symbolized the Zoroastrian supreme deity, Ahura Mazda. Contemporary Zoroastrians, shunning idolatry, consider it to be a representation of the human spirit. During the twentieth century, the* fravahr *became a symbol of Iranian nationalism and is frequently used in jewelry, clothing, wall hangings, and even bumper stickers by Zoroastrians and non-Zoroastrian Iranians alike.* Photo by author.

ongoing Greek-Persian political rivalry is that most of the subject populations occupying this never-ending battleground were neither Greek nor Persian. Year after year, the farmers, craftsmen, and tradespeople of Anatolia, Mesopotamia, Egypt, the Levant, and the Caucasus were forced to provide services or give up their crops, daughters, and living quarters to an endless rotation of occupying foreign armies. Tribal nomads were somewhat better off, since they often constituted the main fighting forces and could simply switch sides or go home.

Also, the lines between the Greek and Persian armies were not so clearly drawn. Greeks were assigned governorships in some western Persian provinces, and Greek soldiers and even commanders served in the Persian army. During Xerxes I's invasion of Greece, some two-thirds of the Persian army was made up of Greek mercenaries. More important, not all Greeks and not all Persians were soldiers and occupiers; many were simply settlers who integrated over time into local society and were as much victims of the winds of war as anybody else.

> THE ACHAEMENID EMPIRE
> 559–330 BCE

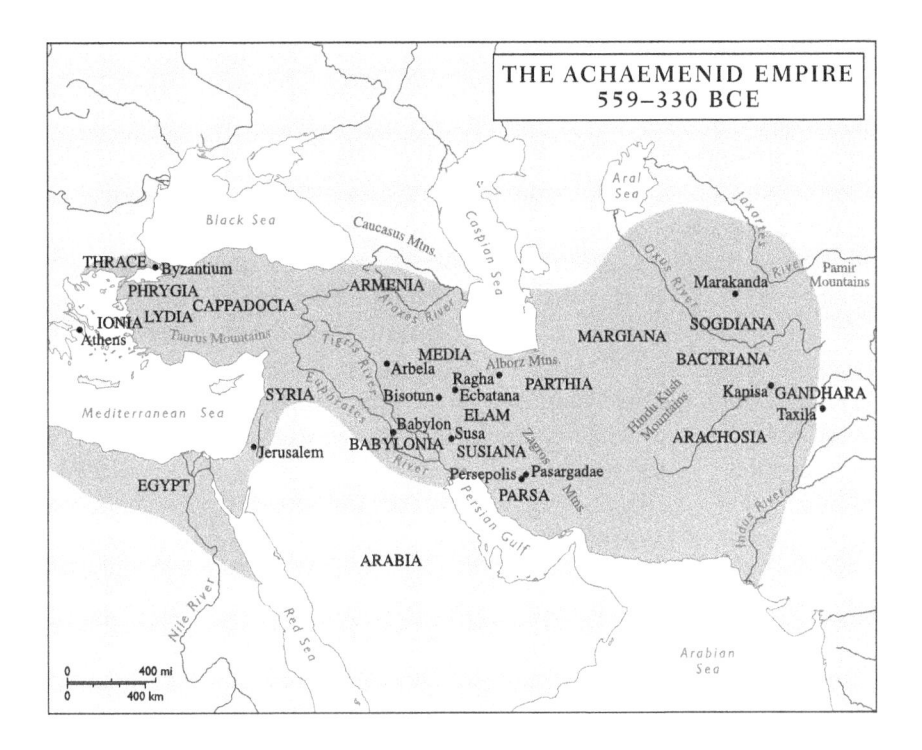

As common inheritors of the patriarchal Indo-European tradition, neither the Persian nor the Greek male elites had much to say about women, and what they did say was usually not positive. The Persepolis fortification tablets provide some information about women workers: in unskilled professions they were allotted one-third less food rations than men, although for skilled workers the rations were equal; new mothers were given extra rations, but more if they had boys. Royal Persian women could own estates and employ laborers, but in the Greek sources they are mainly portrayed as ambitious schemers instigating court intrigues. The practice of incestuous marriages among the Persian royalty, first noted by Herodotus during the fifth century BCE, is condemned as unnatural by Western writers and sometimes used for ridicule. For example, the first-century BCE Roman poet Catullus insults a rival with the words, "May a Magus be born of the abominable union between Gellius and his mother, and may he learn the entrail divination of the Persians!"[5]

An extraordinary Iranian woman by the name of Mania served briefly as satrap of the province of Aolis in western Anatolia at the end of the fifth century BCE. The Athenian writer Xenophon describes her rule as characterized by "magnificence" (that is, royal generosity), making the apparently counterintuitive point that at least some women were actually capable of demonstrating this quality: "Whenever she came to the court of Pharnabazus she brought him gifts continually, and whenever Pharnabazus went down to visit her provinces she welcomed him with all fair and courteous entertainment beyond what his other viceroys were wont to do. . . . Nor was she sparing of her gifts to those who won her admiration; and thus she furnished herself with a mercenary force of exceptional splendor."[6] Mania's son-in-law, finding it outrageous that a woman should hold such a high position, murdered her.

Subsequent female rulers of Iranian lands were rare and suffered similar fates: short reigns and dismissive mentions by historians. Alexander the Great's Bactrian wife Roxana looms large in legend, but the historical facts of her life are not particularly happy—she was at least considered important enough to have to be murdered along with her son, Alexander IV, so that the usurper Cassander could assume the Macedonian kingship following Alexander's death.

The nomadic steppe societies of the Sakas may have had a somewhat higher regard for women. Saka women participated in battle and provided the source for Greek legends about fearsome "Amazon" warriors. According to Herodotus, the Sauromatian Sakas intermarried with these Amazon women, and "Ever since then the women of the Sauromatae have followed their ancient ways; they ride out hunting, with their men or without them; they go to war, and dress the same as the men."[7] The Massagatae Sakas who defeated Cyrus the Great were ruled by a queen, Tomyris (Tahmrayish); Herodotus lists their chief deity as "Hestia"—his Greek equivalent for a goddess whose actual Saka name is not known. In later centuries, the Turkic peoples who gradually took over the place of the Scythians as masters of the steppe also had strong female characters. Even to the present day, women in the rural Turkic communities of Central Asia—particularly the Kyrgyz and Kazakhs—are more publicly visible and active than in many other traditional Islamic societies.

Weakened by years of infighting and court intrigues, the Persian Empire proved unable to withstand the well-organized armies of Alexander III of Macedon, known as "Alexander the Great" in Western history (Persian sources, not surprisingly, call him "Alexander the Accursed"). Although the entire process actually took twelve years, the Macedonian advance, province by province, proved irreversible and ended with the destruction of Persepolis in 330 BCE. According to the

Greek historian Diodorus Siculus, "The Macedonians spent the whole day in pillage but still could not satisfy their inexhaustible greed. . . . As for the women, they dragged them away forcibly with their jewels, treating as slaves the whole group of captives. As Persepolis had surpassed all other cities in prosperity, so she now exceeded them in misfortune."[8]

Following a successful campaign into India, Alexander himself died prematurely a few years later in Babylon in 323 BCE. The Macedonian conqueror left behind Greek garrisons throughout the empire, many of them in newly built Greek-style towns he named after himself. At least twenty Alexandrias were constructed throughout Western and Central Asia, five of them in Afghanistan alone. (The present-day city of Kandahar is a corruption of the original Greek name.) Much of the Achaemenid administration he left in place, however, along with a number of Iranian provincial governors. Alexander had been criticized within his own army for adopting Iranian dress and customs, in particular for enforcing the Persian practice of prostration by anyone entering his presence.

After his death, Alexander's provincial governors vied to enlarge their respective territories. Ptolemy, the satrap of Egypt, declared independence in 320, establishing a dynasty that would rule until the death of Cleopatra VII in 30 BCE. In 312 BCE, the satrap of Mesopotamia, Seleucus Nicator, followed Ptolemy's example and declared his independence as well. Seleucus used this vital region as a base for expansion both east and west, and soon brought much of the former Macedonian Empire under his control. For the next three centuries his descendants, the Seleucids, administered a Hellenistic state that at its peak included most of the territories where Iranian peoples lived, from Anatolia, the Caucasus, and Babylonia to Central Asia and the Indus Valley.

Seleucus followed Alexander's precedent by taking an Iranian wife, Apama, the daughter of a Sogdian general from Central Asia, thereby introducing Iranian blood into the line of his successors. Throughout the Seleucid period and for some time afterward, Greek settlers lived alongside Iranians and others. They built satellite towns on the Greek model, complete with agoras (Greek-style marketplaces), public theaters, and temples to the various Greek gods who were often conflated with local Iranian ones. This co-mingling is evident in the multireligious nature of the third-century BCE "Oxus temple" at Takht-e Sangin in what is now southern Tajikistan, where both Greek and Iranian deities were worshipped. The so-called Oxus Treasure of magnificent gold artifacts and other precious objects, now housed in the Victoria and Albert and British Museums in London, is believed to have originated from the temple at Takht-e Sangin.

In another example of syncretism from the Seleucid period, Greek sculpture is thought to have stimulated the emergence of Buddhist art in the Gandhara region of northwest India, the meeting ground of Iranian and Indic cultures. In Iran proper, the proliferation of statues representing deities—in particular the goddess Anahita during the time of Artaxerxes II—is attributed to Hellenistic influence as well. A cult of the Greek hero Heracles became quite widespread in western Iran; a statue of him projects from the rock at Bisotun not far from Darius's royal inscription. Farther west, the Seleucid city of Dura-Europos on the Euphrates River (in what is now eastern Syria) was a melting pot of Greeks, Romans, Syrians, Jews, and Persians. In addition to Judaism, Zoroastrianism, and Mithraism, various pagan cults co-existed, each leaving traces in the form of inscriptions and iconography.

Despite the hybrid culture that flourished under the Seleucids, their authority was constantly threatened from all sides. This threat included the increasing power of Rome in the West and that of the Indian Mauryas in the East, as well as frequent local revolts from within. As early as 250 BCE the Greek satrap of Bactria, Diodotus I, declared independence from the Seleucids and established a Graeco-Bactrian kingdom that survived for a little more than a century. Numerous Hellenistic remains have been found at sites in northern Afghanistan, especially at Ay Khanum where the ruins of Alexandria-on-the-Oxus have been excavated. The city's layout is typically Greek, including a theater and a gymnasium—along with an architecturally Zoroastrian Temple of Zeus, further evidence of the blending of Greek and Iranian religion that had taken place in the region.

Both the idea of paradise, conceived as a garden, and the symbol of the halo, which was originally an indication of divine investiture, were transmitted to the West as a result of Persian contact with the Greeks and are attested through countless examples in religion, art, and architecture. These Iranian notions date back at least to the Achaemenid period if not earlier.

The English word "paradise" traces back, through French, Latin, and Greek, to the Avestan term *pairi daeza*, which meant "walled enclosure." Since the ancient Iranians were pioneers in the irrigation of arid lands through their system of underground channels (*qanat*s), it is not surprising that they perceived their gardens as islands of heaven in the desert. The Achaemenids saw the construction of gardens as a way of improving the world, which is a central ethical imperative in Zoroastrianism.

The typical Iranian garden is a quadrangle transected into smaller squares by straight channels of running water. This design (called *chahar bagh* in Persian) can be seen on pottery dating as far back as four thousand years. After the Arab conquests in the seventh century, Muslim settlers built Iranian gardens throughout their new empire, stretching across North Africa and into Andalusia (southern Spain). The Spanish and Portuguese later introduced the Iranian garden design into the Western Hemisphere, where it can be seen throughout Latin America and places such as New Orleans in the United States. Persian carpets often feature complex garden designs—a way of bringing paradise into the home.

Eram ("Heaven") Garden in Shiraz was built in the mid-nineteenth century. The Old Persian term pairi daeza—*adopted into Greek as* paradaisos—*referred to a walled garden, and since ancient times Iranian gardens have served as a metaphor for paradise on earth. The model of the Persian garden, consisting of quadrangles bisected by channels of running water, spread to India, Central Asia, and North Africa, and from there the Spanish and Portuguese took it to the New World.* Photo by author

The symbol of the halo, which like the notion of paradise became highly visible in Christianity and Islam, derives from the ancient Iranian concept of *khvaraneh*, or divine blessing. As early as the Young Avesta around the eighth century BCE, *khvaraneh* is associated with the divine right of kingship. In other words, in Iranian tradition—as in numerous other Indo-European traditions including the English—kings rule as regents of the divine, though not as gods in their own right as in Egypt, for example. If they do not rule justly, this charisma will leave them and attach itself to another.

In Iranian art, *khvaraneh* is symbolized by light radiating around the head of the king. The Greeks and Romans borrowed both the concept (Greek *tyche basileos*; Latin *fortuna regia*) and the symbolism, later leading to the use of halos to signify holy figures in Christianity. Later still, Islamic art represented *khvaraneh* (or *farr*, in modern Persian) not by a golden ring about the head but as fire; it is used to designate prophetic status, adorning images of such figures as Adam, Noah, Joseph, Muhammad, and others.

CHAPTER 3

Parthians, Sasanians, and Sogdians (247 BCE–651 CE)

On November 14, 55 BCE, the Roman general Marcus Crassus set out for the East at the head of a large army. His objective was to crush the Parthian Empire in Iran and thus bring the lucrative Silk Road trade under Roman control. An ambitious man recently returned from Julius Caesar's successful campaigns in Gaul, Crassus refused to listen to critics such as Cicero who pointed out that Parthia was ostensibly an ally bound to Rome by a treaty.

Crassus's hubris would result in catastrophe for Rome: on May 6, 53 BCE, his army of 100,000 was utterly routed by the Parthians at Carrhae (modern Harran in southeastern Turkey), surrounded by a skilled cavalry who rained arrows on the enemy even as they feigned retreat—the so-called Parthian shot. As the first-century Greco-Roman historian Plutarch relates, "the Parthians shot as they fled, and next to the Scythians, they do this most effectively; and it is a very clever thing to seek safety while still fighting, and to take away the shame of flight."[1]

The Battle of Carrhae introduced the Romans to a new and alien form of warfare, that of the Central Asian steppes, for which they were most ill-prepared. The Parthians were master archers and horsemen, descended from the nomadic Parni tribe who had begun to establish independent control over the northeastern Seleucid satrapy of Parthava two centuries earlier. For them, hit-and-run tactics were a way of life.

Originating as a breakaway Seleucid state, the Parthians—or Arsacids, to use their dynastic name—had maintained many Hellenistic traditions. They continued to use Greek for their coinage, where they referred to themselves as "philhellenes" (lovers of Greek civilization). At the same time, the Arsacid house claimed descent from the Achaemenids, adopting the royal Persian title "King of kings" from them. The Parthian administration was highly decentralized, however, and their strength ultimately depended on the continued support of seven powerful families who controlled the various provinces.

In keeping with this light-handed approach, the Arsacids' policy toward their subjects was largely one of non-interference (in religious and cultural matters, for example), as long as taxes were paid and rebellions avoided. Their own religious inclinations are not clear and may have been highly diverse. A number of important individual Parthians seem to have had an attachment to the cult of Mithra, which is not surprising given the ancient Indo-Iranian deity's association with the warrior class. Mithraism spread westward to the Roman army through culturally mixed border regions such as Dura-Europos in eastern Syria and became hugely popular among Roman soldiers stationed as far away as northern England where the remains of a Mithra temple can still be seen today.

Remains of a Mithra temple (Mithraeum) rest in Carrawburgh, Northumberland, England near Hadrian's Wall on the Scottish border. Roman soldiers built over five hundred temples to the Iranian god Mithra all across the Roman Empire from the first through the early fifth centuries. Photo by Camilla Brandt

Mithra is also represented among a group of colossal statues at Mt. Nemrud in southeastern Anatolia, built by an Armenian king of the Commagene dynasty during the first century BCE. The Commagene kingdom vacillated between the Parthian and Roman empires, cast into the unfortunate position of buffer zone between the two. Sometimes nominally independent, sometimes under the sway of Rome, Armenia was often as not a Parthian province, ruled by Parthian governors; even ethnically Armenian officials often had Parthian names. Iranian civilization heavily influenced Armenian culture, notably in religion and ritual. The chief Armenian god in pre-Christian times was Aramazd (the Zoroastrian Ahura Mazda), and the Armenians revered Anahita and Mithra as well.

Apart from Mithraism and Zoroastrianism, non-Iranian religions such as Buddhism, Judaism, and Christianity underwent much of their early development during Arsacid rule. Buddhism flourished in the lands of the Kushan Empire to the east (what is now Pakistan) and spread from there into Bactria and thence eastward along the Silk Road to China. Early Christians, persecuted as an illegal sect in the Roman Empire, found safe haven in the Parthian lands, where they established hundreds of churches and more than twenty bishoprics. Jews were fully integrated into Iranian society by that point, having been a part of it for several centuries; many were active in trade.

Mutual influences between all these traditions were a product of the Parthian Empire's multiculturalism and tolerance. A good example of such influence is the idea of an impending apocalypse, which first appears in the form of a Judeo-Greek text claiming to be an ancient Persian prophecy. This work, the *Oracles of Hystaspes*, was the basis of the Christian Book of Revelation.

The Parthians themselves left no texts to speak of, apart from their coinage. This lack makes it extremely difficult to piece together a meaningful picture of their society. Some later literary works appear to derive from Parthian-era stories, though it is hard to know how much has been added or changed. The epic romance *Vis and Ramin*, versified into New Persian by Fakhr al-din Gorgani during the mid-eleventh century, was apparently a well-known tale in the former Parthian lands of northeastern Iran which had been Gorgani's home.

The Parthian society evoked in Gorgani's poem would have appeared strange and exotic even in his time, a thousand years later. The freedom and assertiveness of the female characters, particularly the heroine, Vis, are striking. She is not unique in this respect, as is clear from the words and actions of other female characters—for example, her nurse who gives her the following advice:

> The well-born women of the world delight
> In marrying a courtier or a knight,
> And some, who have a husband, also see
> A special friend who's sworn to secrecy;
> She loves her husband, and embraces him,
> And then her happy friend replaces him.[2]

The Parthian oral tradition was presumably the basis of what Roman critics labeled the "Asiatic" style—characterized by hyperbole and jewel/flower metaphors—which became popular in the Greek and Latin literature of late antiquity. Gorgani's version of the Vis and Ramin story, transmitted to the West by traders, provided the basis for the medieval French romance Tristan and Iseult.

The Romans' humiliating setback at Carrhae put an end to their dreams of direct access to China. Parthia's control over the Silk Road trade network enriched the empire and established its role as one of the major world powers of the early Common Era. By this time the Romans and the Chinese were well aware of each other's civilizations and eager to engage in trade for commodities. The Parthians, firmly entrenched between the two, were ideally situated to reap the benefits of this commerce.

Parthians and their eastern neighbors, the Sogdians, became the best-known foreign figures in imperial China, not just in the world of business but in other domains as well. Many of the first Buddhist scholars and missionaries to make their appearance in China had Parthian surnames. Collectively, Iranians and other foreigners arriving via the Silk Road were referred to by the derisive Chinese term "Hu," which meant "Western barbarians"; Iranians nevertheless figure prominently in Chinese history well into the Tang period (618–917 CE).

The Parthians, like the Medes eight centuries earlier, were overthrown from within. In a later legend preserved in the *Book of the Deeds of Ardeshir Papakan*, the Parthian king Artabanus (Ardawan) V has a falling out with a young courtier named Ardeshir. This courtier is from the family of Sasan who live at the opposite end of the country, in Parsa, where they are custodians of an important temple to the goddess Anahita. The king's favorite maid falls in love with Ardeshir; she raids the royal treasury and persuades Ardeshir to run away with her, telling him of a prophecy that he will soon become king. Artabanus sets off in pursuit the next day, and along the road he encounters a pair of women who tell him they have seen the fleeing couple followed by a ram. The king's chief priest nervously explains the significance of this: the ram symbolizes the divine blessing of kingship (*khvaraneh*), which has abandoned Artabanus and will attach itself to Ardeshir.

Although the *Book of the Deeds* is not a historical source as such, in 224 CE Ardeshir the Sasanian does indeed defeat Artabanus and bring about the fall of the Parthians. The dynastic transition from the Parthian Arsacids to the Persian Sasanians bears a number of further similarities to the shift from the Medes to the Persians. In both cases, the local ruling house of Parsa (Persia) rises up and overthrows an imperial government of culturally related Iranians, takes over their existing empire, and expands its boundaries. Also, in both cases the new imperial government replaces a loose federal administration with one that is more centralized, systematic, and ultimately more powerful and effective. In another significant parallel, just as important Mede families retained their position under the Achaemenids, Sasanian stability rested on the support of the seven major Parthian clans, all of whom transferred their allegiance to the new regime.

In terms of the dynamics of world history, the establishment of the Sasanian Empire as successors to the Parthians maintained the geopolitical balance between East and West. Successive incarnations of Graeco-Roman versus Iranian civilizations divided West Asia between two great empires, roughly along a north-south axis marked by the Euphrates River. The lands of the Eastern Mediterranean, Mesopotamia, Anatolia, and the Caucasus were border regions that vacillated endlessly between these two hegemonic powers—and, sadly for them, were repeatedly scorched and trampled as the rival imperial armies marched back and forth.

This general framework, which endured for more than a millennium, would persist even after the seventh-century Arab conquests, albeit in an altered form. The bureaucrats, merchants, and craftsmen of the towns had to be constantly alert so as to stay on the side of the winners, while the farmers of the fields were repeatedly forced to supply food, shelter, and women to passing battalions. Nomads, being difficult to pin down, did their best to stay out of the way of imperial forces but often joined up temporarily as mercenaries if they were promised booty.

Iran held the upper hand over Rome throughout much of the third century. Ardeshir's successor, his son Shapur I, began his long and illustrious career with a decisive victory over the Romans in 244. The Roman emperor, Gordian III, was killed during (or shortly after) the battle, and his successor, Philip the Arab, was forced to accept Shapur's terms.

The Roman emperors Valerian and Philip the Arab surrender to Shapur I, who sits erect on his horse. Philip ceded Armenia to Shapur in 244 along with an indemnity of half a million gold coins. In 260 the Roman army under Valerian was roundly defeated at Edessa in northern Mesopotamia; the emperor along with tens of thousands of Roman soldiers and craftsmen were captured and taken to live permanently in Iran, where they were put to work building the new city of Bishapur as well as dams and other infrastructure throughout the country. Naqsh-e Rostam, near Persepolis, photo by Manya Saadi-nejad

In 260 Shapur defeated the Roman army once again, this time capturing Emperor Valerian I and several important Roman officials. Valerian was deported to Iran, along with large numbers of Greek- and Syriac-speaking soldiers, where most spent the remainder of their lives. Roman mosaics—presumably done by Greek artists—have been found at Bishapur (Shapur's City, built by Roman slave labor) in southern Pars, and captive Roman engineers built Iran's first bridge-dam, known as "Caesar's Dam," across the Karun River in the city of Shushtar.

Shapur's reign was also a period of religious ferment, during which several major religions began to assume their definitive shape.

Babylonia, the most productive and populous part of the Sasanian Empire, was a highly cosmopolitan region where multifarious versions of Judaism, Christianity, and local religions were practiced. Within this cultural complex the new, highly syncretistic religion of Manichaeism emerged.

The founder of this new faith, Mani, was an ethnic Parthian, raised in Mesopotamia by his father in an all-male religious commune whose members believed in salvation through special knowledge (Gnosticism) and were staunchly anti-materialist. Their principal ritual was baptism. At the age of twenty-four, Mani founded his own religion, drawing on aspects of Christianity, Zoroastrianism, and the Gnosticism he was raised on. He soon embarked on a mission to northwestern India, where he acquired and incorporated Buddhist-Jainist notions as well. The core of Mani's teaching was the goal of escaping material existence through purification rituals, but he adapted his message to whatever symbols and stories were most familiar to his target audience. "The ancient books have added to my writings," Mani acknowledges in one of his works, but "They did not write nor did they unveil the books the way that I, I have written it."[3]

Mani was able to obtain an audience at the imperial court and win Shapur's protection—indeed, he even seems to have converted several members of the royal family. Thanks to this state support Mani was able to spread his teachings widely by employing a sophisticated network of multilingual missionaries. Manichaeism spread rapidly, not just throughout the Sasanian lands but across the Roman Empire as well. The Roman Catholic theologian Augustine of Hippo spent a number of years as a Manichaean novice before embracing Christianity in his early thirties. Part of Manichaeism's success was that Mani presented his religion not as something new, but as a "perfected" form of whatever religion his audience already practiced, be it Christianity, Zoroastrianism, or Buddhism.

At the time, Christian, Jewish, Zoroastrian, and Buddhist communities were plagued by doubts of textual authenticity and torn from within by theological controversies. Mani cleverly staved off such arguments within his own church by insisting that all true divine scriptures were received directly by him and transmitted to writing by his own hand. Indeed, by creating his own authoritative scriptural canon, Mani was very likely instrumental in forcing other religions to establish unambiguous canons of their own. This consolidation of doctrinal authority had not yet taken place within Judaism, Buddhism, Zoroastrianism, or Christianity, and in each case the field was wide open to whatever teachings individual religious figures chose to propagate. Moreover, most people of the time were illiterate, and ideas traveled by word of mouth rather than via established texts. Mani successfully addressed this reality by adopting the strategy—subsequently taken up by Christianity and Buddhism—of conveying his message through vivid paintings illustrating religious themes, using his unrivaled skills as an artist to reach his largely unlettered audience.

Mani's public popularity and the favor he enjoyed at court raised the ire of the Mazdaean priests, the Magi, who had been lobbying to make Zoroastrianism the official religion of the Sasanian state. Led by the zealous chief priest Kerdir (Kartir), the Magi intrigued endlessly against Mani at court and beyond, but they were not successful as long as Shapur remained alive. Following Shapur's death in 270, however, Kerdir's faction orchestrated the succession of Bahram I who imprisoned Mani and permitted the suppression of his followers. Facing violent persecution in Iran, and soon in the Roman Empire as well, Manichaeism began to spread eastward along the Silk Road. Transmitted to Central Asia by Sogdian merchants, Manichaeism was adopted as the official state religion by the Uighur Turks for almost a century beginning in 763, and it survived in southeastern China as late as the seventeenth century.

Due to the Sasanian Empire's multinational character and unevenly distributed population—which was heavily weighted toward the predominantly Christian and Jewish Mesopotamia in the west—the majority of its subjects remained non-Iranian and non-Zoroastrian even after the Mazdaean priesthood succeeded in crushing the Manichaean threat. Unique for a non-royal, Kerdir left four rock inscriptions throughout the realm, in which he boasts of suppressing all the religions that were present in Iran: "Jews, Buddhists, Brahmins, Greek and Syriac Christians, Baptists, and Manichaeans were struck down, idol temples were destroyed."[4] Kerdir goes on to say that while many of the empire's Iranian subjects still believed in the old deities (*devs*), he turned them to the right path of Mazda-worship. Despite the priest's claims, Zoroastrianism never fully eliminated rival practices even among ethnic Iranians, and competing forms of Iranian religiosity persisted throughout the Sasanian era and beyond.

Because Mani and many other religious figures presented themselves as authentic purveyors of Iranian religion, Mazdaean priests referred not only to Manichaeism but to all manner of alternate teachings as *zandika*, literally "[unauthorized] commentary [on the Avesta]." This terminology makes it difficult to get a true picture of the range of Iranian religions during the Sasanian period, since only the Zoroastrians left texts, and these often do not differentiate between the various "heresies" they oppose. This fact continues to lead scholars even today to lump together a wide range of Iranian religious-based resistance movements as "Manichaean," whereas in fact they were usually something else.

Priestly power during the Sasanian period seems to have been accompanied by a surge in patriarchal attitudes. In the Middle Persian Zoroastrian texts, women are described mainly in negative terms, leading righteous men astray and polluting the world through menstruation; the highest virtue to which they can aspire is obedience. Upper-class women could exercise a measure of agency, but commoners were essentially the property of their husbands, with little or no legal capacity of their own.

Women's sexuality was something to be feared and firmly controlled. In the text known as the *Book of Righteous Viraz*, hell is full of unfaithful women suffering unspeakable tortures which are described in vivid detail. According to the Zoroastrian creation myth as taught by Sasanian priests, Ahura Mazda would have preferred not to entrust childbearing to women: "if I had secured a garment wherefrom I could make man, I would never have created thee, whose antagonist is the race of vicious persons."[5] The Sasanian religious texts may reflect a degree of wishful thinking on the part of the priests, but given their power and influence in Sasanian society, one may imagine that women's lives were affected by such misogynistic attitudes.

The association of religion with rival factions at court was a recurring feature throughout the Sasanian period. Kerdir's priestly group continued their ascendancy under Bahram's son and successor, Bahram II, who reigned from 274 to 293. On his death, however, they faced a setback with the accession of Narseh (reigned 293–302), who sought to restore the ruling family's religious authority as custodians of the cult of Anahita. A rock relief at Naghsh-e Rostam near Persepolis depicts Narseh receiving the diadem of kingship from this important goddess. Narseh also ended his two predecessors' policies of persecuting Christians and Jews.

Sasanian dealings with Christians, and to a lesser extent Jews, were complicated by several often conflicting considerations. Prior to the Roman emperor Constantine's legalization of Christianity in 313, Christians fleeing the Roman Empire could find refuge in the Iranian lands, where they often flourished. As the Byzantine (Eastern Roman) form of Christianity gradually achieved official status, Christians following other sects continued to migrate to Iran. On the other hand, some of Iran's largest Christian communities were mostly captured Romans, who could be seen as potential fifth columnists.

But as Christians and Jews were so numerous, especially in the Mesopotamian provinces, their support was vital to the stability of the empire. As Hormizd IV acknowledged in the late sixth century: "Just as our royal throne cannot stand on its two front legs without the two back ones, our kingdom cannot stand or endure firmly if we cause the Christians and the adherents of other faiths, who differ in belief from ourselves, to become hostile to us."[6]

Due to this ambivalence toward the various communities under their rule, successive Sasanian emperors wavered in their religious policies. Certain rulers sought the support of the Mazdaean priesthood by persecuting other religious communities, while others attempted to diminish the priests' power by giving favorable treatment to non-Zoroastrians. A number of Sasanian monarchs cemented their ties to these communities by marrying the daughters of Christian or Jewish religious leaders. In any case, in contrast to the Roman world, the Sasanians never actually outlawed any religion.

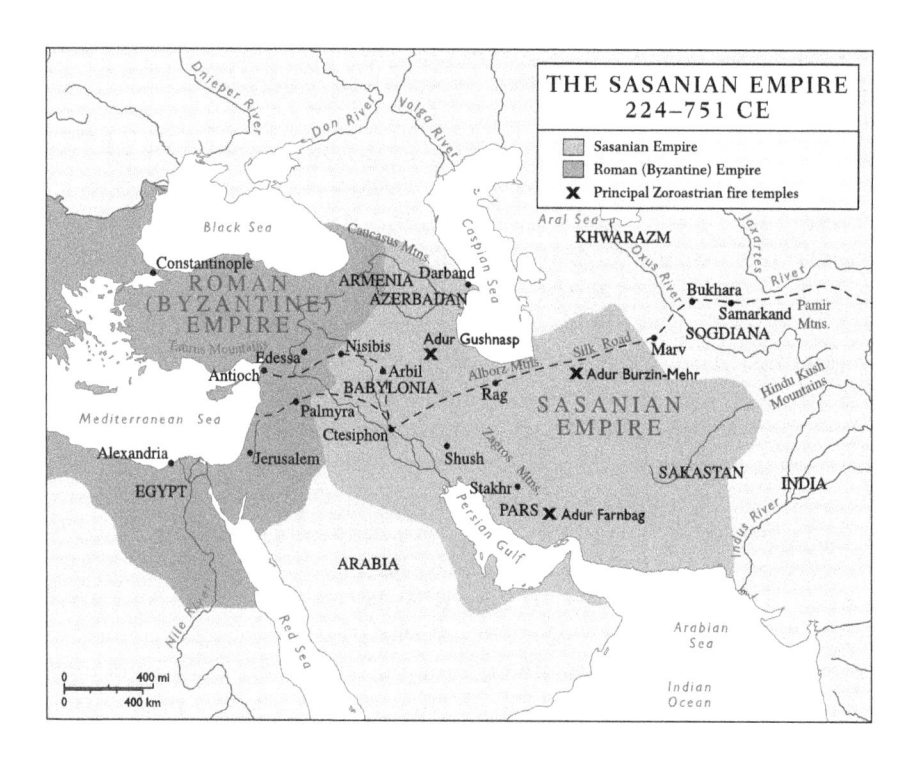

By the latter part of the fifth century, the Sasanian Empire was at a low ebb both politically and financially. The landowning nobility and the priesthood held most of the power and wealth, whereas the largely rural peasant population had suffered greatly from a series of famines. Conditions were ripe for social upheaval, and this came about as a massive reform movement led by a religious figure named Mazdak.

Mazdak, who came from a line of dissenters within Zoroastrianism, preached a form of proto-communism which asserted that human unhappiness was the result of the inequitable distribution of goods, in particular, property and women. (The wealthy of the time were hoarding grain to increase prices and kept massive numbers of wives and concubines.) He therefore called for the opening of both grain silos and harems to the general public.

Mazdak won the support of the Sasanian emperor Kavad I (reigned 488–496 and 498–531), to the horror and outrage of the priests and nobles, who protested that "If women and wealth are to be held in common, how will a son know his father, or a father his son? If men are to be equal in the world, social distinctions will be unclear."[7] In response to this unprecedented challenge to their unique privileges, Iran's elites conspired to have Kavad overthrown, finally deposing him in 496 in favor of his brother. Kavad escaped to Central Asia and took refuge with the nomadic Hephthalites (White Huns, who were probably an eastern Saka group), who helped to him regain his throne two years later. In order to repay the Hephthalites, he attacked their enemies, the Romans, to the west, taking parts of eastern Anatolia and forcing the Byzantines to pay subsidies in exchange for an armistice.

Kavad's death three decades later was followed by another succession dispute, with one faction supporting his social reform policies and the other favoring the interests of the priests and aristocrats. The latter group were ultimately successful, installing their favored son Khosrow I on the throne in 531 and having Mazdak executed along with thousands of his followers.

Khosrow I, known as Anushirvan (the Immortal Soul), has gone down in legend as the greatest of the Sasanian emperors. Ironically, to a large extent his success may have stemmed from his willingness to confirm and systematize some of the economic reforms put into place by his father. He made the tax system on farmers rational by tying it to their fluctuating annual production rather than allowing the unlimited extortions that had previously prevailed. Moreover, he took over direct control of tax revenues, bypassing the prominent landowning families and adding greatly to his own imperial coffers. Making use of his newly available financial resources, Khosrow invested heavily in the improvement of roads and urban structures. He further reduced corruption and interference from among the elite class by giving more power to local landowners, called *dehgan*s, whom he found easier to control.

Khosrow also increased salaries for the military, enabling him to reorganize and strengthen his army. This enhanced military capacity emboldened him to invade Byzantine territory in 540, breaking a treaty of "eternal peace" he had signed with the Roman emperor Justinian a mere eight years earlier. He had been encouraged in this venture by overtures from the Germanic Goths, who had overrun the western Roman Empire during the previous century and now flanked Byzantium on the opposite side from the Persians.

Apart from his military campaigns and massive building projects, Khosrow is known for his patronage of learning and the arts. During his youth he studied philosophy under several Christian teachers. As emperor he expanded the academy at Gondeshapur in Khuzestan; this had started out a Nestorian Christian seminary, but under Khosrow's patronage it became the greatest institution of higher learning of its time.

After the Byzantine emperor Justinian closed the neo-Platonist academy at Athens in 529, a number of Greek academics took refuge in the Sasanian lands, praising Khosrow as the very incarnation of Plato's Philosopher King. Some found employment at Gondeshapur, where the curriculum included philosophy, astronomy, physics, literature, and medicine. Education at Gondeshapur drew on Greek, Indian, Persian, and Mesopotamian scholarly traditions, and in some ways it laid the foundation for modern universities. After the Arab conquests in the seventh century, the school retained its prestige, and many sons of the Muslim nouveaux riches received their education from Christian, Jewish, or pagan professors.

Khosrow cultivated relations with India, from where the game of chess was imported to Iran during his reign. His prime minister, Bozorgmehr, who became the legendary model of the wise advisor, wrote a treatise on the game, and in exchange invented backgammon which was then sent to India. Bozorgmehr is associated with the rise of "wisdom literature," or "mirrors for princes," which became highly popular in the Islamic period.

An example of this literary genre is the book of animal fables known as *Kalila and Dimna*, based on the Indian *Pancatantra* which was introduced to Iran by one of Khosrow's court physicians. These tales, which feature two conniving jackals who act as advisors to the well-meaning but suggestible lion king, are thinly disguised political allegory. In one story the jackals grow jealous of the king's budding friendship with a powerful bull; they poison the lion's ears against his new companion, until he finally relents and kills his blameless friend in a fit of paranoia.

Apart from teaching the principles of justice and political savvy, "mirrors for princes" provided a model for the royal lifestyle, which included hunting and playing polo—an Iranian invention, which spread to India and then much later to England—as well as chess and backgammon. The legendary *Deeds of Ardeshir* offers guidance on appropriate leisure activities, relating that when Ardeshir was still a youth it was "commanded that he should go to the hunt and polo[-field] with his own children and courtiers. Ardeshir did this, [and] with the help of the gods, he proved to be triumphant and more adept than them all in polo, horsemanship, chess, and backgammon and all other knowledge."[8] The advice genre extended to children as well: a Zoroastrian text on proper schooling lists forty-three principles for good students, including the exhortation that "on their way to and from school they should go by the most direct route, and not strike or abuse dogs, chickens, or cows along the way."[9]

Khosrow was succeeded in 579 by his son, Hormizd IV, amid ongoing conflicts with the Byzantines to the west and Central Asian Turks to the east. To the north another Turkic group, the Khazars, had begun raiding Sasanian territory, as had Arabs to the south: the empire was embattled on all sides. Hormizd initially placed his hope in a general named Bahram Chubin, a member of one of the seven powerful Parthian families on whose support the Sasanians had depended since the beginning. The two quarreled, however, and Bahram rose in rebellion.

In response to this threat, in 590 Hormizd was overthrown and killed by two Parthian uncles (on his mother's side), who put his son Khosrow II (also called Khosrow Parvez, "the Victorious") on the throne. Khosrow II then had one of these same uncles killed; at this, the other rebelled and, with Parthian support, had Bahram Chubin enthroned in Khosrow's place. Khosrow escaped to Byzantium, but was restored to power with Byzantine help a year later. Bahram Chubin fled east and was finally assassinated on Khosrow's orders. His power at last confirmed, Khosrow II went on to reign for another thirty-seven years, but the Sasanians' fragile dependence on Parthian support had been exposed.

Khosrow's early reign was crowned by a dramatic expansion into Byzantine territories. Taking advantage of internal disorder within the Roman Empire following the murder of Emperor Maurice in 602, the Sasanian armies moved in and captured much of the Levant and North Africa. In 614, Sasanian invaders captured Jerusalem and carted off the "True Cross" of Jesus Christ to Iran.

Finally under Emperor Heraclius, the Byzantine army, aided by Persian defectors, staged a successful counterattack. In 624, the Roman army managed to penetrate the Adur Gushnasp temple in Media which held one of the three holiest fires in Zoroastrianism. This humiliation drew the outrage of the Sasanian nobility and priesthood, who ceased to see Khosrow as an effective protector of the realm. He survived a few more years as a weak emperor, until a group of Parthian nobles (still pulling strings behind the scene) finally deposed him in 628 in favor of his son Kavad II.

Though not popularly remembered as a great ruler, Khosrow II was immortalized in later Persian literature such as the *Book of Kings* and Nezami Ganjavi's *Khosrow and Shirin*, which recounts the emperor's turbulent marriage to a Christian princess. Iran's most legendary musician, Barbad, was employed at Khosrow's court; he is credited with formalizing Iranian music, and elements of his system survive in Iranian classical music today. Another composer of the time, the harpist Nakisa, was Barbad's colleague and sometime collaborator.

It is said that Barbad was initially barred from court by a jealous rival. One night, however, during a drinking party in one of the royal gardens, music began wafting through the air that was so beautiful it seemed to be coming from heaven. Khosrow demanded to know the provenance of these lovely sounds; it turned out that they were produced by Barbad hiding in a tree. Barbad was hired on the spot, and his rival expelled from the king's entourage.

Khosrow II was executed shortly after being deposed, along with all his male relatives who were potential heirs to the throne. This paranoid gesture on Kavad's part permanently crippled an already weak empire. Kavad himself died after a few months, paving the way for a tumultuous interregnum in which the throne was briefly seized by a Parthian general named Shahrbaraz, then by Khosrow's daughter Borandokht, then by Shahrbaraz's son, then Borandokht's sister, and then by Borandokht a second time—all within the space of three years.

Not surprisingly, Borandokht's second reign was cut short by her murder. Her successor, Yazdegerd III (reigned 632–651), proved to be the last of the Sasanians. Far off in Arabia, a prophetic figure known as Muhammad had proclaimed a new religion, Islam. When news of the goings-on in Iran reached his ears, Muhammad reportedly commented, "A nation that appoints a woman as its ruler shall never prosper."[10]

Iran *was* a prosperous country, of course, which is why the Arabs invaded it a few years after Muhammad's death. Throughout the Sasanian Period, commercial traffic along the trans-Asian trade routes had continued to increase. The principal actors and beneficiaries of this traffic were the Sogdians of Central Asia, whose main city was Samarkand (in present-day Uzbekistan). Their language, an east Iranian dialect, became the lingua franca of the Silk Road as far as China, where Sogdian merchants established expatriate colonies in cities such as Dunhuang, Luoyang, and Chang'an (modern Xian). A large proportion of China's foreign trade depended upon the Sogdians, whom the annals of the Tang dynasty describe as traders by nature: "They excel in commerce and love gain; once a man reaches the age of twenty, he goes off to the neighboring realms; wherever there are profits to be made, they go."[11]

From the time of Alexander's conquests onward the Sogdians were rarely politically independent, but their distance from imperial centers in Iran allowed them a measure of self-determination. On the other hand, their proximity to the Central Asian steppes left them at the front line of defense against incursions from nomadic raiders. At times the Sogdian lands were under the de facto control of nomadic groups such as the Hephthalites and later waves of Turks. But the largely urban Sogdians also had a kind of symbiotic relationship with the nomads, who provided them with trade items such as leather and other animal products while receiving manufactured and luxury goods in return. Also, nomadic individuals or groups often chose to settle in the towns and integrate themselves into urban society, which resulted in their adaptation to Sogdian life.

Sogdians were thus purveyors of culture as well as goods. They were particularly prominent in the transmission of religions, including Buddhism, Christianity, and Manichaeism. None of these religions appears to have become widespread in the Sogdian heartlands, where local Iranian cults continued to predominate (except in the southern regions adjacent to Bactria, which became largely Buddhist). Individual Sogdians, however, adopted these foreign faiths, probably as a way of participating in the long-distance commerce controlled by Buddhists, Christians, or Manichaeans. The development of these religiously affiliated trade networks was tied to the establishment of monasteries, which would give shelter and support to traveling merchants while receiving substantial donations from them in return.

This sixth-century painting of a Sogdian goddess, probably Anahita or Nanai, decorates part of a wall at Panjikent, Tajikistan. Sogdian traders were the principal actors along the Silk Road; many became quite wealthy and commissioned magnificent murals to decorate the walls inside their mansions. The head of the goddess is ringed by a halo, symbolizing divine blessing (kvaraneh)—an artistic element that was borrowed into Christian, Buddhist, and Muslim art. The Sogdian murals from Panjikent and nearby Afrasiab in Uzbekistan are some of the earliest examples of the Iranian painting tradition; most, however, are in poor condition. Photo by author

Sogdian art has left some of the most significant artifacts of the Sasanian era, including metalwork, textiles, and particularly painting. Indoor murals from the homes of wealthy Sogdian merchants in Panjikent (just across the border of Tajikistan from Samarkand) are some of the oldest and most vivid examples of the Iranian painting tradition and shed much light on the culture of the period. The themes illustrated are often recognizably Iranian, including scenes related to stories in the *Book of Kings* and Iranian mythology, but they also show a range of influences from East and West. Chinese motifs can be detected, and one Panjikent painting shows the mythological founders of Rome, Romulus and Remus, suckling at the belly of a she-wolf.

CHAPTER 4

The Iranization of Islam (651–1027)

Abo'l-Qasem Ferdowsi, author of the Persian national epic known as the *Book of Kings*, perfectly epitomizes the conundrum of Iranian identity. A Muslim born and raised, this tenth-century poet considered the Arab conquest to be the tragic ending to Iran's long and glorious history:

> But for the Persians I will weep, and for
> The House of Sasan ruined by this war:
> Alas for their great crown and throne, for all
> The royal splendor destined now to fall,
> To be fragmented by the Arabs' might;
> The stars decree for us defeat and flight.[1]

The sudden emergence of the Arabs as a major geopolitical force beginning in the mid-seventh century is one of the great surprises of world history and continues to be a subject for discussion and debate among historians. This phenomenon is usually associated with the rise of Islam as a new world religion, but the standard view owes something to back-projection. The earliest documented information about Islam dates to decades after its foundation, and the narrative of Islam's first century is based on that constructed by Muslim historians—who were hardly impartial observers—two centuries or more after the fact.

Islamic civilization did not appear all at once; it took shape over several centuries. Many peoples contributed to its development, and among these the Iranians were foremost. Their role is not surprising considering the criteria on which the notion of "civilization" is typically defined: urbanization, political institutions, scientific achievements, literature, and the arts. The Arabs had little of this of their own to build on, whereas Iranians had some twelve centuries or more to draw from.

Islam (which means "submission" in Arabic) is usually thought of as an Arab innovation, and in some respects it was. But the Qur'anic text on which it is based incorporates many pre-existing ideas, Iranian as well as Semitic. Iranians had long lived and traded along the coasts of the Arabian peninsula, so Iranian culture was not unfamiliar to the Arabs. A Persian companion of the Prophet Muhammad, Salman, introduced trench warfare, which was a turning point in the early Muslim community's struggle against their enemies from Mecca—in later Sufi tradition "Salman Farsi" is even said to have been Muhammad's spiritual guide. A story describing a miraculous night journey (*mi'raj*) during which the Prophet visits heaven and hell became widely accepted by Muslims, even though it does not appear in the Qur'an. Its original source would seem to be the Zoroastrian *Book of Righteous Viraz*; the Muslim version would later inspire Dante's *Divine Comedy*.

During the first decades of the Arab conquests, Islam was considered to be merely an aspect of Arab identity, "the Arabs' religion" (*al-din al-'arab*). In order to become a "Muslim" (literally, "one who submits"), a non-Arab had to have an Arab patron who would provide him with membership in an Arab clan. The Arabs often resisted this patronage, since increasing a clan's membership meant distributing booty and other benefits more widely. At the same time, these very benefits motivated many non-Arabs to seek entrance into the Arab-Islamic community, the *umma*.

Muhammad died in 632, the same year the eight-year-old Yazdegerd III acceded to the Sasanian throne in Iran. Muhammad's military career was limited to Arabia, but by 636 his followers began their conquest of the Sasanian Empire, which they absorbed entirely within a decade. This remarkable feat continues to amaze students of history, just as it still baffles and saddens many Iranians themselves. How could a people living on the very margins of civilization, who had never been more than raiders harassing the borders of the great empires, make such short work of the age-old Iranian state?

Part of the key to understanding the Arab conquests lies precisely in the centrality of raiding in Arab society. While some Arabs in small urban settlements like the town of Mecca were involved in trade (and this included Muhammad himself), across most of the peninsula the desert economy was based on keeping livestock, and just as in Central Asia, raiding the herds of others was often necessary for a group's survival. In the absence of any central authority, the only form of social control was agreements between tribes, and these pacts were constantly being renegotiated. Muhammad's success in uniting all the Arab tribes under his leadership was unprecedented—and meant that they could no longer raid each other.

Since raiding was a vital component of the Arab economy, the unification of the Arab tribes forced them to extend their forays beyond the peninsula. In this they were spectacularly successful, thanks to their fighting skills and sense of common purpose. The fact that the Byzantine and Sasanian empires had been weakened through long wars against each other as well as by their own internal struggles surely helped the Arab cause, as did the fact that defeated troops often defected to them.

Because the Arabs' motives were largely economic, they focused their energies on conquering established trade routes and commercial centers. The empire they built was initially an urban one; the Islamization of the countryside took centuries. When entering a town, the Arabs' first act was generally to appoint their own supervisor of the central market (Pers. *bazaar*), which was the heart of urban activity and the principal source of revenue for the state. All business transactions were henceforth supposed to follow Islamic norms. This favored Muslim businessmen and served as motivation for non-Muslim merchants to convert.

An additional factor aiding the Arabs' success was that the inhabitants of many towns—especially in Syria and Mesopotamia—welcomed them without a struggle. This is not so hard to understand as these lands were inhabited mainly by Semitic peoples, akin to the Arabs, who had been subjected to more than a thousand years of abuses by Persians and Greeks. The taxes levied by the Arabs were less onerous than those extracted by their predecessors, at least at first, and the Arabs did not interfere with local affairs as long as their sovereignty was acknowledged. There was little attempt to impose Arab culture—including their religion—during this early period. On the contrary, it was the Arabs who were increasingly overwhelmed by pressure from their subjects to allow them to join the ruling class, which they accomplished by becoming clients (Ar. *mawali*) of Arab patrons and accepting their new religion.

The attempt by Iranian bureaucrats and businessmen to preserve their positions by insinuating themselves into the new hierarchy was met with suspicion by many among the Arab elites. The Umayyad Caliph Muʻawiyah wrote in a letter to his governor in Iraq: "Be watchful of Iranian Muslims and never treat them as equals of Arabs. . . . As far as possible they are to be given lesser pensions and lowly jobs."[2]

Although they mistrusted their new subjects, the Arabs' policy of not reinventing the wheel when it came to administering their new empire was base on pragmatism. They had no experience in running a large, unified state and wisely contented themselves with allowing things to continue as before provided their nominal overlordship was respected. In Syria, where the ruling Umayyad family established their imperial capital at Damascus, the prior Byzantine administration was left largely intact. (In fact, later Muslim writers criticize the Arab Umayyads for quickly lapsing into decadent Roman lifestyles.) Within the former Sasanian Empire the same held true, and Iranian institutions remained for the most part untouched. Syrian and Persian officials could hold onto their jobs by finding Arab patrons, with whom they cemented ties by marrying each other's daughters, attending the mosque together, and entering into business partnerships.

Both the merchant and artisanal classes, which had been relegated to the lowest status in Sasanian society—lower even than farmers, since cultivation is seen as a beneficent activity in Zoroastrianism—were relatively quick to seek integration into the new order. Within a matter of decades, so many non-Arabs had taken on Arab patronage that they came to outnumber the Arabs themselves. (This demographic shift within the Muslim community probably occurred early in the eighth century.) The emerging majority of non-Arab client/converts, the *mawali*, were resentful that their reliance on the ongoing support of their patrons made them second-class citizens.

Furthermore, historic rivalries and inequalities persisted among the Arab clans themselves. A small number of Arab families were favored by the Umayyad government with plum jobs and business deals, while others, less fortunate, got sent off to staff lonely garrisons in remote provinces. Since the Qur'an differentiates among humans only in regard to the sincerity of their faith, not only *mawali* converts but large numbers of marginalized Arabs as well came to see Umayyad despotism as fundamentally un-Islamic. The collective dissatisfaction of these dispossessed groups grew into a mass movement that ultimately changed the course of Islamic history forever.

For anyone disaffected by Umayyad rule, a potent rallying force was the emerging but still unformed ideology of Shi'ism. This belief emerged from the conviction that Muhammad's chosen successor, his cousin Ali who was also married to Muhammad's daughter Fatima, had been unjustly deprived of the caliphate following the Prophet's death; the Umayyads were therefore usurpers. (The term "Shi'ism" derives from *shi'at 'Ali*, "the partisans of Ali.") The Umayyads were also seen as having murdered the Prophet's only surviving grandson, Husayn, who stood against them at the Battle of Karbala in 680.

Despite this Umayyad victory, Karbala along with the rest of southern Iraq remained a Shi'ite stronghold, as it still is today, and since that time annual mourning ceremonies commemorating Husayn's martyrdom—representing on some level a continuation of the ancient Mesopotamian Tammuzi myth—have remained central to Shi'ite religious practice. According to a Shi'ite *hadith* (a report regarding the words or deeds of the Muhammad or the Imams), "Every believer, whose eyes shed tears upon the killing of Husayn b. Ali and his companions, such that the tears roll down his cheeks, God shall accommodate him in the elevated rooms of paradise."[3]

Over the subsequent decades further revolts occurred in eastern Iran, far from the Umayyads' Syrian power base. When the Arabs, seeking to bring the Silk Road under their control, conquered Samarkand in 712, the Sogdian elites preserved their position by "becoming Muslim"—literally, they "submitted" (Ar. *aslamu*). However, for the next ten years they rebelled whenever they thought they could get away with it, enlisting Turkish and Chinese support. The Arabs had to send another army to reconquer the region, which they did in 722, but the Sogdians remained restive. The Umayyads faced even greater challenges in the eastern province of Khorasan, where several major rebellions occurred during the late 740s.

The Iranians who rose up against Umayyad rule in the east were mostly either superficially Islamicized or not at all. Many joined the so-called Abbasids, a para-Shi'ite movement that sought to challenge the legitimacy of the Umayyads on the principle that the caliph should be a member of the Prophet's family. (They rallied in the name of a descendant of Abbas, one of Muhammad's uncles.) But this rationale appears to have been mainly symbolic, since the movement attracted not only disenfranchised Arab settlers but also a whole range of local Iranians whose religious affiliations are unclear. Even the movement's military leader, the Iranian general Behzadan known in the Arabic sources as Abu Muslim, was seen by many of his followers as a semi-divine figure in his own right.

More or less simultaneous with Abu Muslim's uprising was another led by Behafarid, whose claim to authority was explicitly Zoroastrian. Ironically, the Zoroastrian priests of the region, threatened by their rival's religious claims, turned to Abu Muslim to quell Behafarid's rebellion and asked their Zoroastrian followers to give him their support. After having Behafarid captured and executed in 748, Abu Muslim went on to challenge the Umayyads directly, defeating them on the banks Iraq's Zab River in 750. The Umayyads overthrown, the new Abbasid caliph al-Saffah moved the capital from Damascus to the Shi'ite stronghold of Kufa in southern Iraq, at the western edge of the Iranian world.

Ironically, but perhaps not surprisingly, the new government quickly shed its Shi'ite ideology in an effort to establish its legitimacy in the eyes of Sunni Muslims, who outnumbered the Shi'ites. Also, fearing Abu Muslim's charismatic popularity, the new caliph appointed him governor of Syria and Egypt to distance him from his support base in eastern Iran. Relations between Abu Muslim and the new government deteriorated, until he was eventually executed. His followers were outraged; some of them even broke off into a new religious sect, claiming him to be immortal and awaiting his miraculous return.

Not all Iranians welcomed the new political order, especially in the wake of Abu Muslim's murder. In 755, a neo-Zoroastrian leader named Sunpadh raised an army with the vow to avenge Abu Muslim by marching on Mecca and destroying Islam's most sacred shrine, the Kaaba. (He was not successful.) Another rebellion, led by a Central Asian Mazdakite known as Moqanna' (the Veiled One) who had been one of Abu Muslim's commanders, was not put down until 780.

The last major nativist Iranian revolt was that of the neo-Mazdakite Babak in Azerbaijan, which lasted from 816 to 837. After eluding government authorities for more than two decades, Babak was finally captured and brought before the Caliph Mu'tasim for judgment. The caliph, seeking to make an example of the rebel leader, had his hands and feet cut off one at a time. Babak surprised the Muslim ruler by rubbing the bloody stumps upon his cheeks, explaining that "I am making my face red so that when my body loses blood, people will not say my face has turned yellow from fear."[4] After Babak's uprising was crushed, with more than 100,000 of his followers killed, rebel movements in Iran tended to take the outward form of Shi'ism; many of these retained certain Mazdakite or Zoroastrian beliefs, however.

The establishment of the Abbasid Empire represented a sea change in the history of Islam. First, it was a victory over Umayyad elitism, putting Arab and non-Arab Muslims once and for all on equal footing. Henceforth Islam would be a universal religion, not an ethnic one. Second, by moving the political center of the empire to Iraq, the Abbasids replaced the Byzantine administrative model favored by the Damasacus-based Umayyads with a Mesopotamian one that preserved in many respects the system of the Sasanians. In 762 they built a new capital, Baghdad (a Persian word meaning "God's gift"), just north of the former Sasanian capital of Ctesiphon.

In fact the new regime adopted the Sasanian administrative apparatus so completely—including government ministries, tax collection, titles, court etiquette, and the patronage of poetry and music—that the Abbasid state could be considered a continuation of the Sasanian Empire in Islamic guise. Military commanders were recompensed for their service by land grants, allowing them to derive their income by extracting revenue directly from those who worked the land. This kind of tax-farming system, which enriched the owners of huge estates even as it impoverished the peasants, survived in various forms well into the second half of the twentieth century.

The social and geographical changes brought about by the Abbasid revolution created new impetus for what would develop into "Islamic" civilization. Even in strictly religious terms, Islam is based on far more than simply the sacred text revealed to Muhammad—just as Christianity is more than the Gospels, and Judaism is more than the Torah. Jesus was a Jew and Muhammad was an Arab, but in the same way that Christian theology and philosophy were produced by Gentile thinkers steeped in the Hellenistic tradition, Islam was shaped by scholars of Iranian, Babylonian, and Syrian backgrounds. Islam, like Judaism, is largely a religion of divine law, and like the Jewish Talmud, the Islamic Sharia, or divine law, was codified primarily by jurists living in the Iranian world.

The Qur'an is often thought of—by Muslims and non-Muslims alike—as containing the totality of the Islamic religion, but this is not the case. It is not a particularly lengthy text, and while it addresses a number of issues explicitly, there is a whole range of matters on which it is silent. Believing the Qur'an to be a form of direct instruction from God, the Arabs quite naturally assumed that any aspect of their social norms not directly altered by the divine revelation must be acceptable in God's eyes. Thus, except where Qur'anic guidance was clear and specific, existing Arab traditions were seen as the ones society should follow, or at least the Arabs thought so.

However, as the demographic balance among people claiming Muslim identity shifted in favor of non-Arabs, the expectation that Arab norms would govern all social interactions became problematic. Non-Arabs can hardly be blamed for feeling that their own traditions, in the absence of Qur'anic injunctions, were no less valid than those of the Arabs, but this expectation resulted in frequent conflicts within the increasingly cosmopolitan Muslim community. The Arabs had a habit of appointing Arab judges (*qadis*) to resolve local disputes, and non-Arabs objected to what they often saw as arbitrary rulings. Students of the Qur'an began to realize the need for a uniform legal code that would serve to maintain social stability within what had become a far-flung and highly diverse empire.

The Qur'an was naturally the first source to which this emerging class of legal scholars, the Ulama (*'ulema'*, literally, "knowledgeable ones") would turn. But since the Qur'an is silent on so many matters, they required additional bases on which to form legal opinions (*fatwa*s). Relying on the Qur'anic verse which states "You have a beautiful model in the Messenger of God,"[5] many sought to support their positions by citing hadiths about the views or behavior of Muhammad during his lifetime. An additional source was reasoning by analogy (*qiyas*), based on examples from the Qur'an and hadiths.

Various Muslim jurists, each with his personal following of students and paying clients, had their own specific approaches. Some of these coalesced into recognized schools, while others faded into obsolescence. Representing the majority of Muslims, the Sunnis (literally, "traditionists") came to accept four schools of jurisprudence, each employing its own particular mix of methods for deriving the Sharia. The Shi'as developed a school of their own, emphasizing the teachings of the Shi'ite Imams. Of the five schools of law, the one founded by the Sunni Iranian jurist Abu Hanifa is the most flexible, relying more on analogical reasoning than the other schools. It is the most widespread school of law throughout the Muslim world today, though ironically not in Iran, where Shi'ism was imposed by force during the sixteenth century.

The two most important collections of Sunni hadiths, the *Sahih Bukhari* and the *Sahih Muslim*, were compiled during the ninth century by Iranian scholars. The need to justify positions not spelled out in the Qur'an was more pressing where Arab settlers were but a tiny minority. Among ethnic Iranians, Muslims did not become the majority in urban areas until at least the tenth century, and in the countryside this transformation took even longer. Meanwhile other religious communities—Zoroastrian, Christian, and Jewish—kept their own legal systems and ran their own affairs.

A major challenge facing Islamic jurists in the early period was the rampant circulation of unverified hadiths. Since anecdotes traced back to the Prophet were the principal means of resolving differences of belief or practice among Muslims, many hadiths were clearly fabricated merely to support one view or another. For Iranians, some hadiths seem to have aimed mainly at defending Iranian customs—like *Noruz* celebrations, supposedly approved by the Caliph Ali—or asserting that many of Islam's Arab founders had married Sasanian princesses.

At the imperial, provincial, and local levels, Muslim governments relied on the support of the Ulama to legitimize their rule (which was not always easy to do in light of the politicians' often un-Islamic behavior).

In turn, rival groups of scholars had to compete for official favor. As with the merchant class, alliances between the families of government officials and religious clergy were often cemented through marriages and joint business ventures. In this way, the temporal and spiritual powers of Muslim society established a symbiotic relationship—a phenomenon still perceptible in Iran today.

Disagreements among scholars were not limited to questions of establishing a legal code. They hotly debated basic theological problems, such as free will versus predetermination, and the use of reason versus revelation. Since many scholars were trained in the peripatetic tradition of ancient Greek philosophy they were sometimes suspected of being insincere Muslims. The physician Rhazes (Mohammad ibn Zakariyya of Rayy), a pioneer in experimental medicine who is credited with the discovery of alcohol in its pure form (ethanol), made no secret that he had no time or use for Islam. The Bukharan philosopher and physician Avicenna (Abu Ali ibn Sina), whose *Canon of Medicine* was taught in Europe's medical schools into the eighteenth century, was likewise a nonbeliever— although when he died his friends, wishing him to receive an Islamic burial, insisted that he had made a deathbed repentance.

Other Iranian scholars took their Islam quite seriously, however. For devout Sunni Muslims, possibly the single most influential figure in history (apart from the Prophet Muhammad himself) is Mohammad Ghazali, whose forty-volume *Ihya' 'ulum al-din* (Vivification of the Religious Sciences) has remained hugely popular over the centuries as a source of religious guidance. Early in his career he gained renown as a professor of theology at the Nezamiyya seminary (*madrasa*) of Baghdad. But after having mastered Hellenistic philosophy only in order to refute it, Ghazali experienced a spiritual crisis in his thirties and retired from public life. "I examined my motive in my work of teaching," Ghazali later wrote in his memoirs, "and realized that it was not a pure desire for the things of God, but that the impulse moving [me] was the desire for an influential position and public recognition."[6] After resigning from his professorship, Ghazali spent a decade in Syria studying under a Sufi master. Eventually he made his way back to his hometown of Tus in Khorasan, where he spent the remainder of his life writing books and teaching a small circle of select students.

Sufism, which is the term for Islamic mysticism, came into being with the first Muslim mystics in the eighth century. (Some even consider the Prophet Muhammad to have been the first Sufi, although the term did not exist at the time.) Hasan of Basra, the son of a freed Persian slave, is considered one of the founding figures of Sufism. According

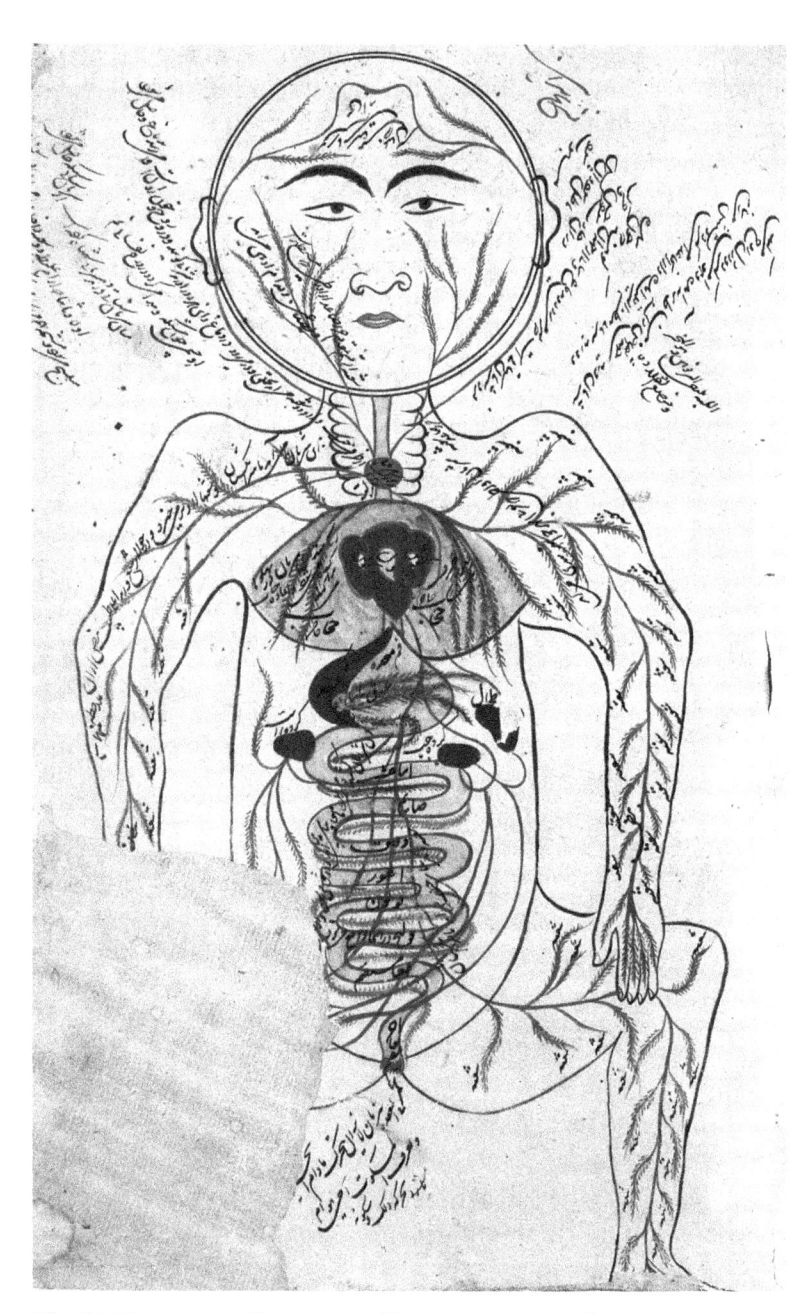

This highly accurate illustration of human arteries and viscera was included in a medieval manuscript copy of the Canon of Medicine *by the eleventh-century Iranian physician-philosopher Abu Ali Sina, known in the West as Avicenna. Avicenna's textbook was translated into Latin and used in the medical schools of Europe well into the early modern period.*
Wellcome Institute, London, Or Arabic MS 155

to popular legend he spent an inordinate amount of time crying; when asked why, he is said to have replied, "For fear that Allah might throw me in the Fire and care less about me."[7]

While some early Sufis were clearly influenced by the asceticism of Christian monks living the deserts of Syria and Egypt, Sufism as a movement took hold farther east under the guidance of Iranian spiritual masters. Bayazid of Bistam is associated with the practice of going into ecstatic trances (*sukr*, or "intoxication") as a means to achieve union with the divine. His teacher was a native of India, and Bayazid's notion of "obliteration in the Ultimate Reality" (*fana'*) bears some similarities to Indian thought. On the other hand, Abo'l-Qasem Jonayd of Baghdad promoted a more "sober" Sufism, based on living in conscious accordance with the divine law.

The most celebrated of all the ecstatic or "intoxicated" Sufis was Mansur Hallaj, an erstwhile student of Jonayd who garnered attention by dancing about in the streets of Baghdad shouting "I am the Divine Truth!" Executed for blasphemy, Hallaj is considered by many Sufis to be the paradigmatic "martyr of love," who willingly suffered death as the price of union with his divine beloved.

Since attraction to Sufi masters usually centered on their personal charisma, they could exercise enormous influence over their followers. Some went so far as to dismiss the Sharia as being an elementary, superficial form of religiosity that could be dispensed with by those who were more spiritually advanced. Such claims put Sufis into direct conflict with the Ulama, who saw themselves as the sole rightful custodians of Islamic spiritual authority. The resulting tensions threatened to pull the developing Muslim society apart, until Ghazali, who was himself both a trained jurist and a practicing Sufi, demonstrated through his work that the two approaches could be reconciled. Essentially, Ghazali argued that the only reliable path to spiritual advancement was not esoteric techniques but merely following the Sharia; simply being a good Muslim would bring one into the direct presence of God.

Scholars of the early Islamic centuries wrote in Arabic because it was the language of scholarship—to refer to all Classical Islamic thinkers as "Arabs" merely because they wrote in Arabic is as inaccurate as calling medieval European scholars "Romans" because they wrote in Latin. These non-Arab scholars deliberately shaped the language to fit their needs, first establishing the rules of Arabic grammar so that they could learn it properly, and then inventing vocabulary to express scientific and abstract concepts the Arabs' desert culture lacked. It is no accident that the most important grammarians of Arabic—notably

Sibawayh of Hamadan—were non-Arabs, since after all it was they who needed to study it as a foreign language.

Most scribes and bureaucrats of the Abbasid administration, as well as high-ranking officials including many prime ministers, were Iranians. During the formative eighth century the Barmak family (the Barmecides), who had originally been Buddhist priests from Balkh, exercised virtual control over the Abbasid government and supported much Iranian cultural activity at court and beyond. Still, because Arabic was the formal language of state, among the elite classes bilingualism was the norm. Since the early caliphs often took Iranian wives, their descendants acquired more Iranian blood with each generation—and given that Muslim children spent most of their early years in the women's quarters, they would have absorbed a fair amount of their mothers' culture as well.

With the shift of gravity toward the Iranian world brought about by the Abbasids, the Iranian scribal class responded to Arab chauvinism by translating literary works from Middle Persian into Arabic so as to ensure their dissemination throughout the whole of the caliphate and demonstrate the superiority of the Persian tradition. Some of these scribes, most notably Ruzbeh "ibn Muqaffa'" (Son of the Shriveled Handed One), were suspected of being not only anti-Arab but anti-Islam as well. (Ibn Muqaffa' was executed as a heretic.) Nevertheless, it is thanks to them that some of the most important works of the Sasanian period survived, their original Persian versions being lost. These literary masterpieces include the *Kalila and Dimna* animal fables and the *Thousand and One Nights*, as well as the Sasanian *Book of Lords* (*Khwaday-namag*) which became the principal source for Ferdowsi's *Book of Kings*.

With literary production limited to Arabic, written Persian largely disappeared for nearly two centuries. From this period only a few scraps of written Persian have survived, including some commercial documents in Judeo-Persian (Persian written in the Hebrew alphabet) discovered in China—evidence of Jewish-Iranian businessmen active along the Silk Road. By the ninth century, however, local Iranian governors in the east had begun to assert their independence, first by refusing to send provincial taxes to Baghdad, then more symbolically by restoring Persian as the official language at court. Yaqub ibn Layth, an uneducated coppersmith by trade who founded the Saffarid dynasty in eastern Iran, reprimanded a sycophantic poet for eulogizing him in Arabic, saying "Why do you recite for me something I can't understand?"[8] Henceforth Yaqub's court poets wrote in Persian.

To the north, the Bukhara-based Samanid dynasty (819–999) went even further in reviving the Persian language. They commissioned

A statue of the tenth-century poet Rudaki, one of the first major figures of New Persian literature, stands in Dushanbe, Tajikistan. Rudaki was a court poet for the Bukhara-based Samanid dynasty, who restored Persian as the official state language after more than two centuries of Arabic dominance. In Tajikistan today Rudaki is considered the father of Tajik literature. Photo by author

Persian translations of Abu Ja'far Tabari's monumental history and Qur'an commentary—the two major works of one of the most respected scholars of his age—since, in the words of the chief translator assigned to the project, "Here, in this region, the language is Persian, and the kings of this realm are Persian kings."[9]

The finest early poets of the newly resurfaced literary Persian, Ja'far ibn Muhammad Rudaki and Abu Mansur Daghighi, enjoyed Samanid patronage. Rudaki's best-known line evokes the homesickness of the soldier on campaign: "Ever comes the scent of the Molian [a stream near Bukhara]/ Ever comes the memory of our beloved friends."[10] It is said that on hearing these lines, the Samanid ruler was so overcome with nostalgia that he immediately turned his army back to Bukhara. Daghighi, for his part, initiated the colossal task (later completed by Ferdowsi) of rendering the now lost Middle Persian *Book of Kings* into New Persian, and many of his lines remain embedded in Ferdowsi's final version of the epic poem.

Yet the original language of the Samanid lands was not Persian but Sogdian, a related but distinct east Iranian tongue. Even as Arabic was being used for official purposes, the general population of Central Asia was becoming not only Muslim but also linguistically Persian, presumably because the Islamic culture they adopted was transmitted to them by Persian-speaking rather than Arabic-speaking Muslims. Thus, Sogdian- and Bactrian-speakers in Central Asia over several generations abandoned their local dialects in favor of Persian, just as Egyptians and Syrians gave up their native idioms for Arabic during the same period.

"New Persian," which is the successor language to the Middle Persian of the Sasanians, is written in a modified Arabic alphabet and contains a large number of Arabic loanwords. The case is similar to English after the Norman conquest in 1066: French became England's administrative language for two centuries, as a result of which a new form of English emerged that was richly impregnated with French. Arabic words in New Persian are pronounced in the Persian fashion, and their meanings often differ significantly from their connotations in Arabic. As Islam spread across Asia among the Turks, Indians, and others, languages such as Turkish and Hindustani (which was split into the Urdu and Hindi dialects for political reasons in the nineteenth century) likewise absorbed huge Perso-Arabic vocabularies as well as the Persian script.

Thanks to the importance of Persian literature as a cultural marker from the time of Rudaki onward, the Persian language has remained stable enough that Iranians today can read works from a thousand years ago with little difficulty. The greatest literary monument of the New Persian language is Ferdowsi's *Book of Kings* (*Shah-nameh*), which he compiled and versified over the course of thirty-one years from oral and written traditions available to him at the time. Consisting of over 60,000 rhymed couplets, the *Book of Kings* tells the legendary history of Iranian monarchs and heroes from the creation of the world up to the Arab conquests.

The main hero in the *Book of Kings* is Rostam, an invincible warrior who lives for nine hundred years and defends the throne for a long succession of Iranian rulers, usually against their archenemies in Central Asia, the "Turanians." The *Book of Kings*' most popular story is a tragedy in which Rostam unwittingly confronts his own son, Sohrab, in battle and kills him, realizing too late what he has done. Hearing or reading the final scene never fails to move Iranians to tears, even though they all know the story by heart:

> [Rostam] lamented, "O young conqueror!
> Alas for your face and stature!
> Alas for your manliness and wisdom!
> Alas for this sorrow and heart-rending loss
> From your mother distant and by your father killed!"[11]

Although Ferdowsi was at least nominally a Muslim, his main goal in producing the *Book of Kings* was to glorify Iran's pre-Islamic past. The work ends in disaster, with Iran's glorious civilization being utterly destroyed by the barbarian Arabs. Ferdowsi deliberately shunned Arab loanwords, striving to make his Persian as "pure" as possible. In this respect the *Book of Kings* perfectly sums up the essential ambivalence at the center of Iranian cultural identity: Iranians for the past thousand years have been overwhelmingly Muslim, yet Islam came to them by means of a humiliating conquest at the hands of a people they despised.

CHAPTER 5

The Turks: Empire-Builders and Champions of Persian Culture (1027–1722)

On his raids into India during the first half of the eleventh century, the Turk warlord Mahmud of Ghazna was accompanied by an Iranian scholar named Abu Rayhan Biruni, who had this to say about the inhabitants of the subcontinent:

> the Indians entirely differ from us in every respect . . . they totally differ from us in religion, as we believe in nothing in which they believe, and vice versa . . . in all manners and usages they differ from us to such a degree as to frighten their children with us, with our dress, and our ways and customs, and as to declare us to be devil's breed, and our doings as the very opposite of all that is good and proper.[1]

Apparently to the eyes of this Muslim writer from Khwarazm, nothing could be more strange and exotic than the peoples of South Asia. And yet, a thousand years later, this very same region is home to one-third of the world's Muslim population, double that of all the Arab countries combined. What brought about this astonishing transformation?

Over the course of eight centuries following Mahmud's incursions, the Indian subcontinent came to be increasingly dominated by Turkic dynasties of Central Asian origin who brought with them a highly Persianized form of Islamic civilization. This included the Persian language itself, which remained the primary idiom of administration well into the nineteenth century under the British Raj (colonial rule which lasted from 1858 to 1947). Throughout this long period much of India's bureaucracy was staffed by immigrants from Iran, who were readily hired by the Turkic ruling class. The relationship between the Turks and Iranians was not unlike that of the Greeks and the Romans: like the Greeks a thousand years before, the Iranians gradually lost their penchant for empire-building by the tenth century, and like the Romans who absorbed the Hellenistic world into their growing empire, the Turks used their superior military skills to take up where the Persians had left off, all the while assimilating and adapting many aspects of Persian culture into their own.

In fact, Turkic-speaking peoples have played a major role in Iranian history, ruling the country from the eleventh century up to the early twentieth. Even today they represent more than a quarter of Iran's population. Originating from eastern Siberia, the Turks first appear in historical records as raiders attacking lands stretching from China to Iran several centuries prior to the Common Era. In many if not most cases, however, nominally Turkic nomadic confederations were multiethnic and included other groups as well. They share much culturally with the Iranian Sakas but also with the Huns, Mongols, and other steppe peoples with whom they frequently mixed. Since the linguistically and culturally Iranian urban oases of the Silk Road represented their first line of encounter with settled societies, from ancient times successive Turkic groups fell under the influence of Iranian civilization even as they often dominated it politically.

Whether as merchants or warriors, Turks who were active along the Silk Road learned to speak Sogdian, and later on Persian which replaced it as Central Asia's commercial lingua franca. An Lushan, a general in the Chinese army who led a rebellion against the Tang government in 755, was born of a Sogdian father and a Turkish mother (his Chinese name is a somewhat inaccurate translation meaning "Rokhshan, the Parthian").[2]

By the end of the first millennium, Turkic dialects were beginning to displace Iranian ones in eastern Central Asia, and the linguistic Turkification of Central Asia has continued steadily ever since. Notwithstanding the unrelenting encroachment of Turkic languages, Iranian cultural norms remain prevalent throughout Central Asia, the Caucasus, and eastern Anatolia even today. Perhaps the most visible sign of this influence is the Iranian new year, *Noruz*, which continues to be celebrated enthusiastically by a wide range of peoples from the Balkans to India.

In fact, the nomadic and settled peoples of Central and Western Asia, broadly though not entirely associated with Turkic and Iranian spoken idioms, have maintained a symbiotic relationship for at least the past three thousand years. Often hostile, this relationship was also one of mutual dependence. The nomadic peoples obtained most of their manufactured goods from the urban settlements bordering the steppes, either through trade or by force. The settled peoples, for their part, depended on the nomads for things like horses and other livestock, as well as animal products such as milk, cheese, and leather. Also, they relied on the steppes to provide them with slaves, which they obtained either through purchase or in battle. Turkic-speaking slaves were prized for their skills as warriors and made up much of the governmental armed forces as well as the private militias of wealthy landowners.

These slave soldiers often became close to their owners, even to the point of serving as their lovers. (Salacious jokes about Mahmud of Ghazna and his beautiful slave boy Ayaz are told even today.) On occasion they might rise up and overthrow their masters, thereby not only attaining their own freedom but sometimes even taking over as the new ruling class. So-called Mamluk (slave) dynasties of Turkic origin ruled eastern Iran (the Khwarazm-shahs) from 1077 to 1231, northern India from 1206 to 1290, and Egypt from 1250 to 1517.

Whenever nomadic peoples chose to settle in urban areas—which they often did as conquerors—they were faced with a public relations problem. The sedentary population perceived them as barbaric and uncivilized, so they had to demonstrate their worthiness to become an accepted part of polite society. They did this by adopting Iranian cultural norms. This meant acquiring a taste for Iranian dress, food, social etiquette, music, and above all the Persian language and its literature. From the ninth century onward, it also meant asserting an Islamic identity, which they often did with the showy zeal of the recent convert.

By the tenth century, centrifugal forces had considerably weakened the central authority of the Baghdad-based Islamic caliphate, with numerous provinces establishing varying degrees of de facto independence. Even in Baghdad, the caliph had fallen under the political hegemony of the Buyid family, originally from northern Iran, who controlled the central Islamic lands from 934 to 1062. The Buyids were Shi'ites, as were the Fatimid dynasty that ruled Egypt during the same period. Thus, during the tenth century, much of the Muslim world was under Shi'ite rule.

Since most Muslims were Sunni, the fact of Shi'ite political dominance became an ideological weapon used by newly converted Turkic groups who promised to restore Sunni governance. The first Turkic leader to do so with success was Mahmud, son of Sebuktegin, a Samanid slave soldier from the city of Ghazna in what is now southeastern Afghanistan. (Like many Arab and Turkic military men, Mahmud's father had married a Persian woman, so he was in fact half-Persian.) Taking advantage of a Samanid state weakened by attacks from a Turkish confederation in the east, the Qara-Khanids, Sebuktegin had assumed control of Khorasan, which was then seized by Mahmud in 998.

From his base in Ghazna, Mahmud launched what would be the first of seventeen raids into northern India. A Shi'ite Fatimid ruler controlled the Punjab at the time; Mahmud attracted popular support through the use of pro-Sunni propaganda. He succeeded in annexing the Punjab to his territory, and through subsequent raids he forced many of northern India's Hindu kings to become his vassals.

Although a small Muslim state had existed in the northwestern part of the Indian subcontinent since the mid-eighth century, it was only beginning with Mahmud's incursions that Islam seriously began to take hold in South Asia. Despite his Turkish warrior credentials, Mahmud, like subsequent Turkic Muslim invaders, was a patron of Persian culture—though the honorarium he offered Ferdowsi for completing the *Book of Kings* was disappointingly small. In the wake of Mahmud's conquests, over the centuries to come it was a highly Persianized form of Islam that penetrated South Asia.

In 1027, Mahmud turned his attention toward the west and took central Iran from the Shi'ite Buyids, again capitalizing on his claim to be a restorer of Sunni Islam. He died three years later, and almost immediately the Ghaznavid state he established was challenged by a new wave of Turkic invaders from Central Asia, the Seljuks.

Like Mahmud's father Sebuktegin, the Seljuks were originally soldiers in the service of the Samanids of Bukhara. Following the fall of the Samanid dynasty at the hands of the Turkic Qara-khanid federation in 999, the Seljuks began to seek a power base of their own, and by 1037 they had wrested much of eastern Iran from the Ghaznavids. They went on to take western Iran from the Ghaznavids as well, and in 1055 they took Baghdad from the Buyids, which established them as the dominant power in the Islamic world.

Seemingly unstoppable, the Seljuks conquered the Christian Caucasian states of Georgia and Armenia in 1064, bringing them face-to-face with the Byzantine Empire for control of Anatolia. In 1071 they defeated the main Roman army at the Battle of Manzikert, opening the way for the Turkization of Anatolia and laying the linguistic foundations for modern-day Turkey.

The actual number of Turkish soldiers was small relative to the general population, and one way they integrated into society was by marrying local women, mainly Greeks and Armenians. Turkization, therefore, was primarily a linguistic phenomenon. Linguistic shift in Anatolia was a slow process, not really completed until after World War I. It was accompanied by Islamization—in an Iranian form, especially at first—with Persian serving as the language of the Seljuk administration. The process of religious conversion took centuries as well: as late as 1914, Christians still constituted more than one-third of the population of the Ottoman capital, Istanbul.

In Iran, the Seljuks established their capital at Esfahan, where they built important monuments such as the congregational mosque which remains functional today. Their prime minister, Hasan of Tus (known as Nezam ol-Molk, or Orderer of the Realm), set up a system of seminaries, called *nezamiyya*s, and also reformed the army and the tax system. Socially, however, he was a strong supporter of the status quo. As he writes in his *Book of Government*: "The king's underlings must not be allowed to assume power, for this causes the utmost harm and destroys the king's splendor and majesty. This particularly applies to women, for they are wearers of the veil and have not complete intelligence."[3]

Promoting the Seljuks' pro-Sunni policy, Nezam ol-Molk also persecuted Shi'ites. This prompted attacks from suicide killers of the Shi'ite Isma'ili sect which controlled impregnable mountaintop fortresses in Iran and Syria. These "assassins," as they were known (from the Arabic *hashishiyyun*, or "hashish smokers," which they probably were not), were spectacularly successful in targeting anti-Shi'ite figures in the Seljuk administration, including Nezam ol-Molk himself who was assassinated in 1092. The suggestion one sometimes hears today that the Assassins were forerunners of today's suicide bombers is somewhat misleading, since they targeted specific individuals and were careful not to harm innocent bystanders.

The Seljuk mission to suppress Isma'ili Shi'ism was prompted largely by the remarkable successes of Isma'ili missionaries, many of whom were trained at the Al-Azhar seminary in Cairo which had been founded as an Isma'ili propaganda center. (Somewhat ironically, it is now the most respected institution of traditional Sunni learning in the Muslim world.) The Iranian poet-traveler Naser-e Khosrow is credited with introducing Isma'ili Shi'ism to the Badakhshan region in what is now northeastern Afghanistan/southern Tajikistan. To this day, the population of Tajik Badakhshan is almost entirely Isma'ili, and they revere Naser-e Khosrow as the founder of their community.

Like their Turkic predecessors the Ghaznavids, the Seljuks were avid patrons of Persian language and culture. The mathematician-poet

Omar Khayyam flourished during their rule, as did the theologian Mohammad Ghazali, and later, the Sufi poet Jalal od-din Rumi. With its multilayered meanings and possible interpretations, poetry was a way to express all manner of feelings that might deviate from the constraints of orthodox religious thought. Indeed, it was often used as a vehicle of protest against the pat truths supplied by formal religion. Omar Khayyam, who was known and respected in his time as a mathematician and scientist, secretly wrote hundreds of quatrains in which he expressed doubts and even anger about the way God made the world:

> He began my creation with constraint
> By giving me life he added only confusion
> We depart reluctantly still not knowing
> The aim of birth, existence, departure.[4]

For Muslim mystics—the Sufis—poetry was the ideal means to hint at the ineffable depth and intensity of the spiritual experience they hoped to achieve. By the early eleventh century, Sufi poets had begun to establish a wellspring of symbols, terms, and metaphors that would constitute the repertory for Persian poetry of all kinds in the centuries to come.

The central message in Sufi poetry is love, which in all its forms is a reflection of God's love for His creation. Love is a corollary to the human predicament, which is the prideful illusion of separation from the Divine. The Sufi "lover" thus yearns to be re-united with the Beloved, most often symbolized in human terms as the youthful beauty who is distant and unattainable. A stock image for depicting this relationship is that of the rose—attractive, aromatic, but ultimately indifferent and possessing potentially harmful thorns—or the nightingale, who laments through the night for the lover he cannot possess. An even stronger metaphor is the moth irresistibly drawn to the candle flame, by which it will eventually be consumed and obliterated.

Sufis emphasize that our original and natural state of being is one of unity with the Divine; all human suffering is due to our subsequent separation. The poet Rumi—whose translated works have now made him the bestselling poet in the English language—evokes this tragedy in the opening lines of his epic six-volume treatise, the *Masnavi*:

> Now listen to the reed-flute's deep lament
> About the heartache being apart has meant:
> "Since from the reed-bed they uprooted me
> My song's expressed each human agony,

> A breast which separation's split in two
> Is what I seek, to share this pain with you:
> When kept from their true origin all yearn
> For union on the day they can return."[5]

Following the usual pattern for empires, over time central authority weakened and the Seljuk territories became increasingly fragmented. Throughout the twelfth century Seljuk states had to contend not only with the Frankish Crusader presence in the west, but also raids from the Qara-khanids and others in the east.

The next and greatest wave of nomadic invasions from Central Asia was led not by Turks but by Mongols, who spoke an unrelated language but whose culture was similar to that of the Turks in many ways. After Genghis (Chinggis) Khan united the Mongol tribes in 1206, many Turkic clans as well joined his army. Throughout Genghis Khan's lifetime, the Mongol-Turkic confederation expanded their control through a series of military campaigns, taking on the Chinese in the east and Iranians in the west. From 1218 to 1221 they brutally crushed the region of Khwarazm (present-day Turkmenistan and Uzbekistan, at that time still Iranian-speaking), opening the way to the conquest of Iran. By the time of Genghis's death in 1227, the Mongol-led nomadic confederacy controlled a huge swath of land from the Caspian Sea to the Korean peninsula.

Genghis's successors continued his unprecedented military successes, pushing ever farther into China, Russia, and Iran. His grandson Hülegü led the Iranian campaign, first dislodging the Isma'ilis from their mountain strongholds—something no previous army had been able to do—then overrunning Baghdad and putting a formal end to the already decrepit Abbasid Caliphate in 1258. Hülegü continued from there into Syria, where the Mongol advance was finally halted by an army from Mamluk Egypt at the Battle of 'Ain Jalut in 1260.

Hülegü made his capital at Tabriz, establishing the Il-khanid dynasty which ruled there until 1335. Perhaps three-quarters of the steppe nomads who participated in the Mongol invasion of Iran stayed on, along with their flocks. This led to overgrazing and competition with local herders and farmers, who complained that the newcomers' livestock were damaging their crops. Many of the nomads turned to brigandage, a problem that persisted throughout rural Iran into the early twentieth century.

The first Il-khans were shamanistic—that is, they relied on the trance-induced insights of shamans for their religious guidance. But under

Il-khan rule, Tibetan Buddhists and Nestorian Christians—whose missionaries were active in the Mongols' Central Asian homeland—enjoyed many privileges and flourished at the expense of Muslims, especially in cities like Tabriz and Arbela (modern Erbil, in Iraqi Kurdistan).

Hülegü brought a number of Chinese scholars to Iran. These imported academics worked with Iranian scientists such as the astronomer Naser od-din Tusi, who oversaw the building of a highly sophisticated observatory at Maragheh in Iranian Azerbaijan. The so-called Pax Mongolica opened up trade along the Silk Road as never before, leading to an unprecedented level of commercial and cultural exchange between East and West. In 1294, the Buddhist Il-khan ruler Gaykhatu introduced the Chinese concept of paper currency to Iran, from whence it spread to Europe.

With Christians and Buddhists occupying the most privileged positions, Muslims chafed under Mongol rule. Hoping for a change in policy, they succeeded in bringing Gaykhatu's nephew Ghazan Khan to the throne in 1295. As a result of Muslim support, Ghazan, who had been raised as a Christian, converted to Islam. Thus, after a brief interlude of a few decades, Iran came once again under Muslim rule. Buddhists and Christians fell out of favor and were subjected to severe reprisals by the majority Muslim population.

Jews fared somewhat better, particularly after one of their community, the physician Rashid od-din Fazlollah, was appointed prime minister following a nominal conversion to Islam. Among his other achievements Rashid od-din composed a universal history of the world, the *Jame' ot-tavarikh*, which is one of the main primary sources for the Mongol period.

The Mongol invasions devastated Iranian civilization in many ways, and a number of cultural centers such as Marv, Balkh, and Nishapur never recovered from the onslaught. On the other hand, once their rule was firmly established, the Mongols became great patrons of Persian culture, and several of Iran's most celebrated poets lived during that time. The family of Jalal od-din Rumi fled their hometown of Balkh while he was still a child, resettling in Anatolia beyond Mongol reach. In Nishapur, the Sufi poet Farid od-din Attar was among those who perished during the Mongol attacks, but in the southwestern city of Shiraz, Mosleh od-din Sa'di managed to escape before the Mongols arrived—although at a later point he was captured and sold into slavery, and subsequently ransomed himself by marrying his owner's ugly, ill-tempered daughter.

Sa'di's tumultuous life informed his irreverent and often cynical work, the *Rose Garden*, which, containing enough pithy sayings to suit almost any possible occasion, may be the most quoted work in all of Persian literature. One of Sa'di's more optimistic stanzas has been enshrined in the Hall of Nations at the United Nations building in New York City:

> Human beings are members of a whole,
> In creation of one essence and soul.
> If one member is afflicted with pain,
> Other members uneasy will remain.
> If you have no sympathy for human pain,
> The name of human you cannot retain.[6]

By the end of the thirteenth century, the Mongol Empire had degenerated into four separate khanates. In China Khubilai Khan founded the Yuan dynasty; the Golden Horde ruled Russia and the steppes, and Western Iran was under the control of the Il-khans. Central Asia, including many eastern Iranian lands, was part of the Chaghatay khanate, ruled by the descendants of Genghis Khan's second son, Chaghatay. Beginning in 1363, many of the western Chaghatay lands were taken over by a Turkic warlord of the Barlas tribe, Timur, known in the West as Tamerlane.

Timur's stated aim was to restore the empire of Genghis Khan. He married a Chinggisid princess as a way of tapping into Mongol legitimacy, taking the title of *göregen*, meaning "son-in-law."[7] At the same time, as a nominal Muslim he adopted the propaganda approach of the Ghaznavids and the Seljuks, claiming the status of "holy warrior" (*ghazi*) fighting in the service of Sunni Islam. Like his predecessors, though, he wore his religious affiliation lightly. In the words of one of his contemporaries, the historian Ibn Arabshah: "He destroyed right custom and went forth wicked with insolent swords that moved hither and thither. He destroyed kings and all the noble and learned, and strove to put out the light of Allah and the Pure Faith. . . . He threw children upon the fire as if burning incense, he added to fornication the drinking of wine."[8]

Establishing his capital at Samarkand, Timur brought the neighboring Turkic and Mongol tribes—some of which had accepted Islam and others of which had not—under his control. One of these tribes was the Uzbeks, who are singled out in Timur's official chronicles as being particularly backward and in need of being subdued. (Ironically, in Uzbekistan today, Timur has been made into a national hero, the "father of the Uzbeks.")

Once having brought much of Central Asia under his control, Timur began a campaign against Iran which lasted from 1383 to 1385. During this time he terrorized the population by mass killings, after which he would build towers out of the severed heads of his victims. In 1398 Timur moved southeastward into India, sacking Delhi which was ruled by another Turkic dynasty of Central Asian origin, the Tughluqs. Almost immediately, he then turned his attention toward the recently established Ottoman Empire that had succeeded the Seljuks in Anatolia, and then to the Mamluks, yet another Turkic dynasty, who ruled Egypt.

Many of the Turkic nomads that had come to occupy Anatolia since the Seljuk victory at Manzikert joined Timur's forces, resentful of Ottoman attempts to impose their authority. These Anatolian nomads were known as Turkmen—Persian for "Turkic"—and their fierce independence would make them a formidable force for helping to support regime changes over the centuries to come.

In 1400 Timur, asserting his status as "holy warrior," conquered the Christian provinces of Georgia and Armenia and killed or enslaved much of the population. Next he invaded Syria, then Baghdad in 1401. The following year Timur defeated the Ottoman army at the Battle of Ankara, capturing the Ottoman sultan Bayazid I and creating the illusion in the minds of many Europeans that he wished to "save Christianity"—an absurd fantasy, given his treatment of Christians in the Middle East. With the western lands effectively subjugated, Timur once again turned to the East with the aim of gaining China. He contracted a fever en route, however, and died in the Central Asian town of Otrar in 1405.

Though Timur spent most of his life waging military campaigns, he used the fruits of his successes to build up Samarkand into the most spectacular city of its day. He was a passionate builder of monuments, commissioning a huge palace for himself at his birthplace of Shahr-i Sabz, south of Samarkand, as well as a massive memorial to his wife, Bibi Khanom, in Samarkand itself, and another to the Sufi master, Ahmad Yasavi, in the town of Turkistan (in today's southern Kazakhstan), in addition to his own mausoleum, the Gur-i Amir in Samarkand.

Timur's architects pushed the limits when it came to size and in some cases exceeded them. The 120-foot cupola of the Bibi Khanom mosque collapsed almost as soon as it was erected, as did the colossal entry arch at Timur's palace in Shahr-i Sabz. Nevertheless, Timurid architecture, most notably its vaulted domes, provided the model for some of the world's most impressive monuments, including the Royal Mosque in the central Iranian city of Esfahan and India's Taj Mahal.

Timur encouraged trade with Europe, and European diplomats and businessmen were amazed by Samarkand's wealth and splendor. Timur's achievements, along with his barbarity, remained firmly entrenched in the European imagination, as seen in English plays by Christopher Marlowe and Nicholas Rowe, operas by Georg Friedrich Handel, Antonio Vivaldi, Josef Mysliveček, and Giacomo Puccini—and even a poem by Edgar Allan Poe.

Timur was less interested in literature than architecture, and a popular legend has him challenging the poet Hafez of Shiraz—whom many consider the most sophisticated of all Iran's great literary figures—on the basis of a couplet in which Hafez writes, "If that Turkish beauty would take our heart in hand/ For the black mole on his (or her) cheek we would exchange Bukhara and Samarkand."[9] Timur, according to the story, objected that these cities were not Hafez's to give, to which he replied, "It is that very arrogance that has brought me to the lowly state in which you see me now."

In accordance with steppe tradition, upon Timur's death his lands were divided up among his descendants. In the absence of a strong, unifying central authority, the various regions asserted their own autonomy under local governors, each with its own personal militia. Timur's son and successor, Shah Rukh, moved his capital to the eastern Iranian city of Herat (now in western Afghanistan) in 1409, but Samarkand retained its wealth and importance throughout much of the fifteenth century. Leaders of the Naqshbandi Sufi order, most notably Khwaja Ubaydallah Ahrar, became politically powerful during this period. Unlike many other orders that shunned politics, the Naqshbandis believed that pious men should associate closely with those in power so as to "make them better Muslims."

Shah Rukh's son Ulugh Beg was a skilled mathematician and astronomer. As governor of Samarkand he oversaw the construction of an advanced observatory that enabled him to create the most accurate map of the heavens since Ptolemy of Alexandria in the second century. In 1417, Ulugh Beg founded a seminary that still stands in Samarkand's main square, the Registan; in keeping with his personal interests, its curriculum emphasized mathematics and astronomy. He established an important library around the same time.

Ulugh Beg was also a patron of literature and the arts, as was his cousin Sultan Husayn Bayqara who ruled the Timurid rump

Noon prayers are held at the shrine of Yaqub Charkhi, a politically active fifteenth-century Sufi saint who was head of the Naqshbandi order founded by the Bukharan Sufi Baha od-din Naqshband a century earlier. The Naqshbandis remain a politically potent force today, especially in countries such as Iraq and Pakistan. In Tajikistan and Uzbekistan they have been instrumental in reviving Islam's popularity during the post-Soviet period; scenes such as this well-attended prayer session would have been rare during Soviet times. Photo by author

state from Herat during the latter decades of the fifteenth century. Sultan Husayn's court included such luminous figures as the poets Abd or-Rahman Jami and Ali Shir Nava'i, as well as the painter Kemal od-din Behzad. Jami is generally held to be the last of the great Classical Persian poets. Nava'i, who wrote in both Persian and Chaghatay Turkish, is considered by today's Uzbeks as the "father of Uzbek literature." Behzad, for his part, is heralded as history's finest painter of Persian miniatures.

Uzbeks brought about the end of Timurid glory, at least in Central Asia. They expelled the Timurid governor of Samarkand, Babur, in 1505, and conquered Herat two years later. The Uzbeks followed the established pattern in acting as patrons of Iranian culture, supporting poets writing in both Persian and Turkish, as well as painters working

This miniature painting in the Safavid style shows a pair of royal lovers with an attendant. Such paintings, which took months to produce, were commissioned to illustrate manuscripts for royal or aristocratic patrons, and were a symbol of power and wealth. Painting by Manya Saadi-nejad, based on a sixteenth-century original by Mohammad Yusuf of Esfahan in the Persian miniature tradition. They also built some of Central Asia's most important monuments, including two of the three seminaries now framing the Registan Square in Samarkand, the Shir-Dar (Lion-Bearing, completed 1636) and the Tilla-Kari (Gold-Work, completed 1660).

As for Babur, he set up his capital at Kabul, from whence he spent the next two decades launching raids into northern India. After conquering Delhi in 1526, Babur decided to stay, becoming the founder of the so-called Mughal[10] dynasty which lasted until 1857. Babur wrote a fascinating memoir, the *Babur-nama*, in Chaghatay Turkish, which is sometimes referred to as the first autobiography by a Muslim writer. It is deeply personal and filled with nostalgia for his lost Central Asian homeland. His descriptions of India, by contrast, are less than flattering: "Hindustan is a place of little charm. There is no beauty in its people, no graceful social intercourse, no poetic talent or understanding, no etiquette, no nobility or manliness."[11]

Under Babur's grandson Akbar the Great, the re-located Timurid Empire in India would grow into the richest and most powerful state in the world, visited and envied by European traders from Portugal, England, France, and Holland. This wealth also attracted a wave of talented individuals from Iran, intensifying the Islamization and Persianization of India that would continue into the twentieth century. Though Muslim sultanates had been in place in Delhi since the eleventh century, it was only under the Mughals that Perso-Islamic culture spread to the general population in a major way, in part through government land grants to Sufi masters whose personal charisma attracted large followings of villagers.

While the Mughal elite retained a sentimental attachment to their Central Asian homeland, with the gradual displacement of long-distance trade from the Silk Roads to the Indian Ocean the Uzbek-ruled lands of Central Asia (broadly referred to as "Turkestan") lost their central importance in the global economy, and what remained of Turkic culture among the Mughals was mostly for show. They liked to hold ceremonies in tents, for example, though these tents were lavish to an extent one can scarcely imagine—massive in size and embroidered with gold thread and intricate designs. In his Persian-language memoirs, the Emperor Jahangir felt it necessary to boast in the early seventeenth century that "I am not ignorant of how to speak or write Turkish."[12]

In fact, the Mughal administrators were mainly ethnic Iranian immigrants or the children of Iranian mothers, and the elite culture was Persian. Government records were kept in Persian, court poets composed their verses in Persian, Iranian musicians worked with Indian

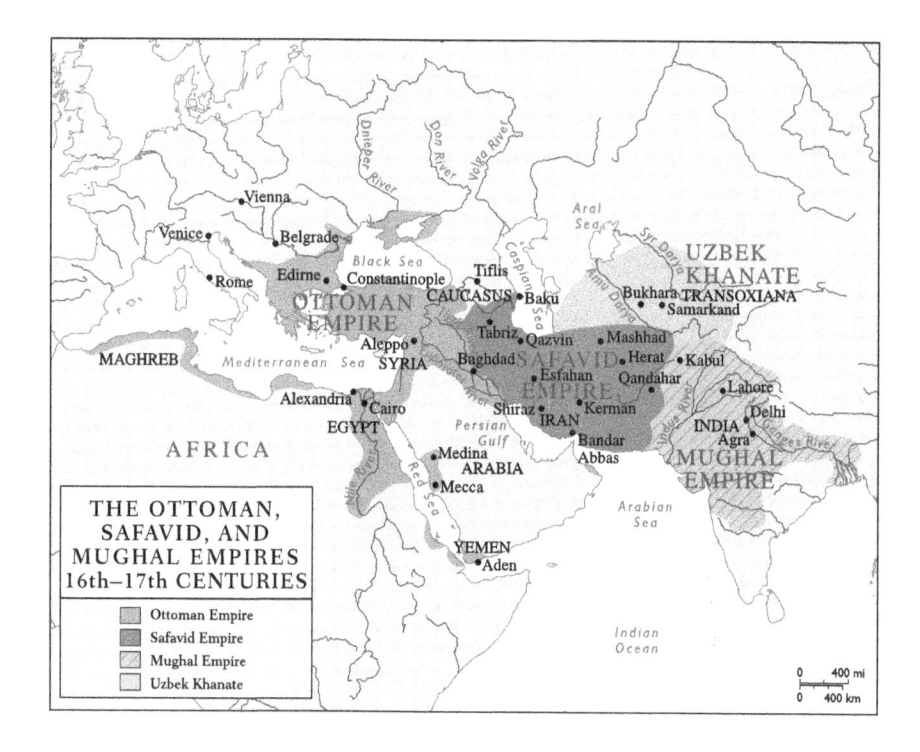

THE OTTOMAN, SAFAVID, AND MUGHAL EMPIRES 16th–17th CENTURIES

- Ottoman Empire
- Safavid Empire
- Mughal Empire
- Uzbek Khanate

colleagues to create the new genre known as "Hindustani music," and painters imported from Iran ran the royal ateliers staffed by local artists. Together with the Safavids, their contemporary rivals who ruled in Iran, the Turkic Mughals of India presided over the greatest expansion of Persian culture in all of history.

While Timurid rule remained in place in eastern Iran throughout the fifteenth century, western Iran during the same period was dominated by Turkmen tribes of nomadic origin, first the so-called Black Sheep confederation (Qara Qoyunlu) from 1406–1468, then the White Sheep (Aq Qoyunlu) up to the end of the century. With their capital at Tabriz, the Turkmen rulers drew their military support from bands of independent-minded nomads living throughout Azerbaijan and Anatolia.

These nomadic groups had been only superficially Islamicized, and they retained many aspects of their original shamanistic culture. They considered the first Shi'ite caliph, Ali, to be a divine figure. This has led some scholars to refer to them as Shi'ites, but it would be more accurate to simply attribute them with "shi'izing tendencies," since their beliefs were quite heretical by orthodox Shi'ite standards. Nevertheless, Shi'ite symbolism was very effective in mobilizing them against the Sunni Ottomans.

Being unlettered and unschooled in any formal Islamic legal tradition, the Turkmens were easily impressed by the charismatic authority of Sufi masters. One Sufi brotherhood which had been established in the region since the late thirteenth century was the Safavids, originally a Sunni order that moved toward Shi'ism as a way of appealing to their restive Turkmen following. The latter were known as *Ghezelbash*, or "red heads," because of their distinctive turbans wrapped around a pointed red crown. During the second half of the fifteenth century the Safavid order became increasingly militarized, and by 1501 their young leader, a remarkable fourteen-year-old by the name of Esma'il, was able to capture Tabriz and assume for himself the ancient title "Kings of Kings of Iran."

Over the subsequent decade, the youthful Esma'il, at the head of a Ghezelbash army that believed him divine and invincible, extended his power from Anatolia and Mesopotamia to eastern Khorasan as far as the Uzbek-held lands. At the Battle of Marv in 1510, Esma'il defeated the Uzbek ruler Muhammad Shaybani Khan, whom he executed and whose skull he had fashioned into a drinking cup in the ancient steppe tradition.

Esma'il's successes alarmed the Ottomans, who forcibly relocated many of his Turkmen supporters farther west into Ottoman lands where they would be easier to control. In 1514, the Ottoman sultan Selim I marched on Azerbaijan at the head of a huge army, engaging the Safavids on the plain of Chalderan. With their superior numbers and European artillery, the Ottomans defeated Esma'il's forces, demolishing the myth of his invincibility. Psychologically devastated and discredited among his formerly devoted followers, Esma'il entered a long retirement that ended with his early death in 1524. His final legacy was the commissioning of a magnificent illustrated copy of the *Book of Kings*, which was completed during the reign of his son, Tahmasp.[13] Many art historians consider this work to be the pinnacle of Persian painting.

Since Tahmasp was only ten when his father died, the reins of government were initially held by his Ghezelbash regent, an able general named Ali Beg Rumlu who managed to suppress the internecine clan rivalries that threatened to tear the new empire apart. On attaining maturity, Tahmasp proved a capable ruler, upholding the Safavid state in the face of constant threats from both the Ottomans in the west and the Uzbeks in the east over a fifty-two-year reign. He moved the capital to Ghazvin, out of reach of the Ottomans, and oversaw the gradual conversion of much of Iran to the "Twelver" branch of Shi'ism which facilitated the rise to political power of the Shi'ite Ulama.

Safavid prestige was enhanced by their success in restoring northern India to the Mughal ruler, Babur's son Humayun, who had been ousted in 1540 by marauding Afghans (a term which at the time signified ethnic Pushtuns, contrary to the broader meaning it has today). Humayun sought refuge at Tahmasp's court and, following an opportunistic conversion to Shi'ism, he was given use of a Safavid army with which he reconquered Delhi in 1555. As Tahmasp had become something of a religious fanatic by that point, many Iranian writers and artists followed along with Humayun to seek new careers under the Mughals. This initiated a two-centuries-long brain drain that culturally depleted Iran, to the great benefit of India.

"Shi'izing" propaganda had played an important role for the Safavids in mobilizing the support of Turkmen warriors, especially against the Ottomans, but their unorthodox beliefs were not Shi'ism per se. In a poem aimed at rallying his warriors, the young shah Esma'il had said of Ali, "Know him to be God, do not call him human"[14]—a clearly heretical view by any standard.

In Tahmasp's time, actual scholarly Shi'ite authority in Iran was still thin on the ground, which meant that the shah had to import legal experts from Lebanon and elsewhere to buttress the legitimacy of the new state. It became government practice to renumerate religious scholars with land grants, as had traditionally been accorded to military leaders. Many religious families thus acquired large estates, which accounts for the impressive landholdings and massive wealth enjoyed by a number of powerful religious figures in Iran even today.

Needless to say, the view of Shi'ism promoted by the Lebanese Ulama differed considerably from the Ali-worshipping folk religion of the Turkmens. Orthodox Shi'ism had to be imposed through government force, first directed at the heretical Ghezelbash and then at the general population, most of whom were Sunni. These forced conversions had little impact in eastern Iran, which led to a permanent political divide between the Persian-speakers of Iran proper and those of modern Afghanistan, Uzbekistan, and Tajikistan, most of whom have remained Sunni to this day.

Upon Tahmasp's death the various Ghezelbash clans renewed their rivalries. These continued throughout the short reigns of the next two Safavid kings, Esma'il II and Mohammad Khodabandeh. Khodabandeh's sixteen-year-old son forced him to abdicate and assumed the throne as Shah Abbas I in 1587. The young Abbas wasted no time in restructuring the increasingly ineffectual Safavid military, which had recently lost much of the Caucasus to the Ottomans and the eastern provinces to the Uzbeks. He hired two English advisors, the brothers Robert and Anthony Sherley, to reorganize his army on the European model, with a salaried officer corps and modern artillery. With this new, professional standing army at his disposal, Abbas was no longer dependent on the tribal Ghezelbash or subject to their internecine intrigues.

In 1598 Abbas moved the Safavid capital from Ghazvin to Esfahan, which was closer to the geographical center of the empire. He then embarked on a massive building campaign, importing Armenian craftsmen from the town of Jolfa on the Araxes River in the Caucasus. "New Jolfa," on the south bank of Esfahan's Zayandeh River, remains a distinctly Armenian neighborhood to this day, and Armenian silver-workers, tile-makers, and other craftsmen continue to be visible figures within the Esfahan bazaar. Of ancient West Asia's many linguistic and ethnic groups, the Armenians are almost unique in having maintained their distinct identity up to the present.

Under Shah Abbas, Armenians also flourished as international businessmen, building up thriving commercial networks that connected Iran with Europe, India, and China. The Armenians were especially important in the traffic of luxury items such as silk. Georgians and Circassians from the Caucasus, meanwhile, attained prominent posts in the government and military. Abbas cultivated relations with European powers, particularly England and Spain, in an effort to circumvent and undermine the political and economic strength of the Ottomans. He offered trading concessions to European companies and allowed Christian missionaries to operate in Iran, though these were allowed to proselytize only among Iran's Christian communities and could not target Muslims. As a result of this missionary activity, a substantial number of Iran's Chaldean Christians and some of its Armenians accepted the pope's authority and became Catholics.

European travelers marveled at the changes brought by Abbas to his new capital, reflected in the expression "Esfahan is half the world." The central urban layout of the city—including the immense Royal Plaza (*Maydan-e Shah*, now *Maydan-e Khomeini*; also known as *Naghsh-e jahan* square) with the Royal Mosque at one end and the entrance to the central bazaar at the other—dates to Shah Abbas's time.

This urban design reflected the growing connection between the merchant class and the Shi'ite Ulama linking economic power with spiritual authority. Among other things, the religious establishment relied on bazaar merchants to fund the construction of mosques and seminaries. This alliance between two powerful social classes would become central to Iran's economic and political life over the coming centuries and is still operative today.

Naghsh-e Jahan Square in Esfahan was built by orders of Shah Abbas I. Shaykh Lotfollah mosque is on the left, the Royal Mosque center-right, and Ali Ghapu palace to the right; the entrance to the main bazaar is behind the viewer, opposite the Royal Mosque. The square, which evolved from the ancient Iranian garden model, is considered by many the pinnacle of urban design throughout the Muslim world. Pascal Xavier Coste, Monuments modernes de la Perse mesurés, dessinés et décrits (Paris: A. Morel, [1867])

The royal palace known as the Ali Ghapu (Grand Gate) stands on the western side of the maydan, facing the delicate Shaykh Lutfullah mosque on the east. Farther west of the Ali Ghapu a four-mile tree-lined avenue, the Chahar Bagh, stretches south to the Zayandeh River, which is crossed by the Allahverdi Khan Bridge, also known as the Bridge of Thirty-Three Arches.

While international commerce flourished under Abbas, it fell increasingly into the hands of Europeans, especially the Indian Ocean trade that linked Europe with India and China. Abbas was able to take the Persian Gulf port city of Gambron from the Portuguese in 1616, renaming it after himself (Bandar Abbas), but the Persian navy was no match for the English or the Dutch. With the decline of the Silk Road, overland trade shifted to a northwest-southeast axis, linking Iran with Muscovite Russia on the one hand and Mughal India on the other. Indian merchant communities grew throughout Iran as a result.

Abbas was succeeded by a series of weak rulers, most of whom were addicted to opium and rarely left the harem. The resulting power vacuum was filled by court intrigues, usually instigated by royal women, and increasingly by the Shiʻite clergy under the leadership of the chief cleric (*shaykh ol-eslam*), Mohammad Bagher Majlesi. Majlesi used his power to suppress all competing forms of religious authority, especially the Sufi orders, illuminationist philosophers who saw truth as light, and rival clerics of the Akhbari school who relied on traditions rather than innovative thought. (Majlesi's group, the Usulis, favored a flexible approach to jurisprudence, which gave more freedom of interpretation to clerics such as himself.) Majlesi also oversaw the closing down of taverns, cafés, and brothels, as well as the banning of opium smoking, gambling, public music and dancing, and sodomy—an exercise in social control that eerily foreshadowed the Islamic revolution of 1979.

The political role of the Usuli clerics persisted up to the time of the last Safavid ruler, Soltan Hossein (reigned 1694–1722). A few years into his reign Soltan Hossein turned over power to his great-aunt and her cohort, retreating like his predecessors into the sex-and-drugs life of the harem. Revolts arose throughout the empire in response to his weak rule. In 1722, an Afghan army laid siege to the Safavid capital, Esfahan.

CHAPTER 6

Under Europe's Shadow (1722–1925)

Father Tadeusz Jan Krusinski, a Polish Jesuit missionary who lived through the Afghan seige of Esfahan in 1722, describes the scenes of horror suffered by the city's starving inhabitants: "Shoe-leather being boiled was for a time the common food; at last they came to eat human flesh, and the streets being full of carcasses, some had their thighs cut off privately . . . several children were stolen and eaten, half dead as they were of famine."[1]

After six months of starvation and misery, a tearful Soltan Hossein finally emerged from the city gates of Esfahan and personally capitulated to the Afghan leader Mahmud Ghilzai. After the fall of the capital, Iranian Shi'as were severely persecuted by their Sunni Pushtun conquerors. In the west as well, the Ottomans took advantage of Iran's turmoil to seize territory and enslave Shi'ite "heretics."

Meanwhile in the north, the Russians under Peter the Great captured Iran's Caspian seaports including Darband, Baku, and Rasht. The Portuguese and Dutch were vying for control of the Persian Gulf, both soon to be elbowed out by the British. The population of Esfahan, which had numbered more than half a million in Shah Abbas's time, fell by a factor of ten to fewer than fifty thousand. In the absence of any kind of strong central authority, the country's various nomadic tribes bickered and fought over grazing lands and raided passing caravans with impunity, disrupting the economy.

Amid the widespread chaos of the 1720s a young Ghezelbash warrior, Nader Gholi Beg of the Afshar tribe, put together a tribal alliance that managed to take control of Khorasan. By 1729 he had become powerful enough to dislodge the Pushtuns from Esfahan, and he went on to push back the Ottomans and Russians, eventually recovering most of the former Safavid territories. Nader's military successes, which were due to a highly disciplined officer corps and the effective use of modern artillery, led to a brief restoration of nominal Safavid rule, but in 1736 he put an end to this charade and had himself crowned king.

Two years later, Nader Shah, who saw himself as a second Tamerlane, launched an invasion of India. In early 1739 his army sacked the Mughal (that is, neo-Timurid) capital of Delhi. The booty they brought back to Iran included the so-called Peacock Throne, a major symbol of Mughal power and wealth, as well as the fabulous Kuh-e Nur—literally "mountain of light"—then the world's largest diamond. (The Peacock Throne thereafter vanished, perhaps melted down for its jewels. The Kuh-i Nur is part of Queen Elizabeth II's crown, and is on display in the Tower of London.) So vast was the plunder from Nader's India invasion that he was able to suspend taxation in Iran for the next three years. In 1740, Nader Shah conquered the Uzbek-controlled khanate of Bukhara: this was the last time the Persian-speaking regions of Central Asia would be under the same government as the rest of Iran.

With both Sunnis and Shi'as represented within his army, Nader Shah put aside the Safavids' religious intolerance. This policy provided a temporary respite for Iran's Sunnis, Christians, Jews, and Zoroastrians. He also modernized the army, equipping ordinary soldiers with rifles and formal training, and even started a small navy based in the Persian Gulf. Stability was short-lived, however, as Nader slipped into mental illness and local tribal-based revolts broke out in response to the reimposition of taxation to finance his unending military campaigns.

In 1747, Nader Shah was assassinated by a group of his own officers, plunging Iran once again into a period of anarchy as regional tribal leaders each asserted their independence. The country's population at this time was as much as 50 percent nomadic, which in the absence of a powerful king made any kind of centralized control virtually impossible. This situation would continue into the early twentieth century.

The constant upheavals of the first half of the eighteenth century in Iran are vividly illustrated in the life of Khadijeh Soltan Daghestani, an aristocratic poet of Esfahan who was successively married off to a series of five different men. Beginning with the Afghans, with each new regime she suffered the execution of her husband of the moment and was forcibly remarried to one of the conquerors. And yet, throughout the whole ordeal she was in love with her childhood sweetheart, a cousin. She followed him to India after the death of her fifth spouse, but died on the way. In one of her surviving poems,

Khadijeh likens her experience to that of the mythical tragic lovers Layla and Majnun:

> Should you hear the tale of my suffering,
> You will forget that of Layla and her story;
> Should you hear of my cousin's love,
> You will forget all about the legend of Majnun.[2]

The year of Nader's assassination, one of his Pushtun officers in the east, Ahmad Khan Abdali of the Durrani tribe, crowned himself "King of Afghanistan," thereby laying the foundations for the modern state of that name. Prior to that time the terms "Afghan" and "Pushtun" had been synonymous, referring to the stubbornly independent tribal peoples of the eastern Hindu Kush who had resisted foreign domination since the time of Alexander the Great. ("Afghan" derives from the Persian word *awghan*, which like the Greek *barbar*—hence "barbarian"—referred to people who speak gibberish: literally, "those [who talk by] saying 'awwwgh'.") The warlike Pushtuns, who speak an east Iranian dialect, may have descended at least in part from the ten "lost" tribes of Israel, who were dispersed into eastern Iran by the Assyrians in 722 BCE. Pushtun cultural values are expressed through the code known as *pushtunwali*, which is based on the principles of hospitality to visitors, the granting of asylum, and the taking of revenge.

Historically, "Afghanistan" simply designated the region inhabited by Pushtuns; under Ahmad Shah, it became a country. The new state he established came to include not just the Pushtun lands but also the regions of Kabul, Herat, and Mazar-i Sharif (Balkh) which remain Persian-speaking to this day. With the Tajik areas of Bukhara, Samarkand, and Khojand farther north falling again under the control of the Uzbeks (who, like the Pushtuns, were Sunnis), the divide between the mostly Sunni eastern Persian-speakers and the mainly Shi'ite west became permanent. Major exceptions include the Sunni Baluch, who inhabit southeastern Iran as well as adjacent parts of southern Afghanistan and southwestern Pakistan, and the Hazaras of central Afghanistan, who are ethnic Mongols but speak Persian and follow the Twelver Shi'ite faith.

With the breakup of the Afsharid state following Nader Shah's assassination in 1747, the Uzbek military reasserted its control in Central Asia, eventually establishing the Emirate of Bukhara in 1785 in the name of a Mongol noble of the Manghit tribe, Shah Murad. Central Asia by this time was largely bilingual, with the Tajik dialect of Persian continuing to dominate urban life and government administration.

The Bukharan state, along with the newly created Afghanistan to the south, found itself increasingly caught between the colonial aspirations of the Russians to the northwest and the British in India. The nineteenth century would be characterized by the intrigues of these two European empires, a geopolitical power struggle that came to be known as the "Great Game."

While Ahmad Shah was consolidating his new polity in the east, in the Caucasus the Christian state of Georgia declared independence from Iran as well. In the southwestern Fars region, yet another of Nader Shah's former generals, Karim Khan Zand (who was of Lor or possibly Kurdish origin), established local control and set up his capital at Shiraz. Like his late ex-employer, Karim Khan initially installed a Safavid puppet ruler, whom he soon dispensed with in 1760. He did not take the title of shah, however, preferring instead to call himself "the People's Advocate" (*vakil or-ra'ya*).

Karim Khan's reputation as one of the most enlightened rulers in Iranian history is summed up in the following observation by British Ambassador Sir John Malcolm in 1815: "The mode which Kareem Khan took to attain and preserve his power, was different from that pursued by any former monarch of Persia. He made no effort to gain strength by the aid of any superstitious or religious feelings. He neither tried to attach his army by gratifying their lust of plunder; nor courted the applause of a vain-glorious nation by the pursuit of ambitious projects or the gorgeous display of royal splendor. He was modest, even to his attire; and though his rule was always firm, his general manner to the meanest of his subjects was familiar and kind."[3]

Karim Khan's rule saw the flourishing of Shiraz, which had been home to the medieval poets Sa'di and Hafez. Many of the city's most important surviving monuments, including the Vakil bazaar, the Vakil mosque, the Vakil bathhouse, and the Karim Khan citadel, date to this period, as does the main part of Sa'di's mausoleum. A distinctive school of art emerged under Zand patronage, in which the influence of European techniques such as foreshortening is increasingly evident. With the establishment of a British trading post at Bushehr on the coast of the Persian Gulf, Iran's connection to the global sea trade was revived, to the benefit of the local economy.

Unfortunately, upon Karim Khan's death in 1779, his successors were unable to maintain the stability of the Zand state against constant attacks from its neighbors and internal struggles from within.

The Turkic Ghajar tribe, based in the city of Sari in northeastern Iran, were the most troublesome. Their chief, a mean-tempered eunuch by the name of Agha Mohammad Khan who had spent sixteen years in Shiraz as a Zand hostage, escaped in 1779 and fled north to take over leadership of the clan.

Agha Mohammad Khan moved the Ghajar capital from Sari in Mazandaran to Tehran, which at the time was merely a village between the Alborz foothills and the ancient city of Rayy. Over the following decade the Ghajars managed to steadily expand their rule over adjacent territories, and in 1794 they defeated and captured the last Zand ruler.

With much of Iran's historical expanse now firmly under his control, Agha Mohammad Khan declared himself King of Kings (*Shahanshah*) in 1796. A cruel and ruthless leader, Agha Mohammad Khan had many enemies. In 1797 he was assassinated in his sleep by three of his servants, whom he had condemned to death but somehow neglected to imprison. He was succeeded by his nephew Baba Khan, crowned as Fath Ali Shah, who had been governor of the province of Fars.

Fath Ali Shah ruled Iran for the next thirty-seven years. His reign saw increasing exposure to Europe and European culture. Fath Ali Shah himself is said to have read the entire third edition of the *Encyclopedia Britannica*, which so impressed him that he had himself formally referred to as "Most Formidable Lord and Master of the *Encyclopedia Britannica*." Persian painting under his rule became distinctly Europeanized in style, marked particularly by large-scale royal portraits done in oils. No less than twenty-five portraits of Fath Ali Shah have survived.

In the decades to come, Europeans would become similarly enamored of Persian high culture. Translations of the classical Persian poets became quite popular in the West. The German poet Johann Wolfgang von Goethe modeled his *West-Eastern Divan* on the odes of Hafez, and in England, Edward Fitzgerald's loose translation of Omar Khayyam's quatrains led to the appearance of Omar Khayyam Societies all over the country. Sa'di's highly quotable *Rose Garden* was cited by such Western writers as George Wilhelm Friedrich Hegel, Alexander Pushkin, and Ralph Waldo Emerson.

The Iranian military still lagged behind European standards, however. The Russians took the formerly Iranian province of Georgia without difficulty, and the Ghajar counterattack led to a war that lasted from 1804 to 1813. Recognizing the superiority of Russia's comparatively modern army, the Ghajars sought support first from England and then from France, but their entreaties fell on deaf ears.

An early nineteenth-century portrait of Ghajar ruler Fath Ali Shah and some of his sons, all dressed in heavily bejeweled royal ceremonial attire. Fath Ali Shah's patronage of the arts fostered the emergence of the Ghajar style of Persian painting, which shows increased European influence especially through a more photographic sense of realism and perspective. British Library Add. Or. 1239

Part of the problem was the Ghajar government's inability to exercise full authority over the country's various nomadic tribes, on whom they relied to provide troops. The majority of Iran's population in the early nineteenth century was still nomadic or semi-nomadic and therefore difficult to control; they were usually happy to join a campaign if it looked to be successful but quick to abandon the cause when things went wrong.

The results of the war with Russia were catastrophic for the Ghajars. The Russians managed to advance as far as Tabriz, and in order to reestablish peace the Ghajars were forced by the Treaty of Golestan in 1813 to cede most of their Caucasian provinces to Russia. They attempted to regain these territories in 1826 but were not successful. The Treaty of Turkomanchay in 1828 transferred even more of the Caucasus to Russia, a loss to Iran that would prove permanent. The psychological effect on Iranians was devastating, and likely explains why Iran has not engaged in any military aggression against its neighbors in the nearly two centuries since.

What Fath Ali Shah lacked in geopolitical skills, however, he made up for in virility. He is said to have had no less than one thousand wives and concubines, producing countless numbers of children. To this day it is taken as something of a joke when an Iranian claims "royal Ghajar lineage."

Fath Ali Shah's successor, his grandson Mohammad Shah, was faced with a growing domestic threat in the form of a new millenarian religious movement led by a Shiraz merchant named Seyyed Ali Mohammad. Iran's Shi'ite society was ripe with expectancy a thousand years after the disappearance of the Twelfth Imam, and Seyyed Ali Mohammad acquired a large following who saw him as the returning savior.

Known to his disciples as "the Gate [of Truth]" (*bab*), Seyyed Ali Mohammad claimed to be receiving a new cycle of divine revelation that superseded the Qur'an. His teaching spread throughout Iran, bringing about a backlash from the country's conservative Shi'ite clergy who began to call for his arrest. In 1847, Mohammad Shah ceded to the clergy's demands, ordering Seyyed Ali Mohammad's confinement and eventual imprisonment in Azerbaijan. Undaunted, the Bab's close disciples continued to spread his teachings.

One of the Bab's principal acolytes was an exceptionally bold woman named Fatemeh Baraghani. Born in 1817, she was a poet also known by her pen name Tahereh and by the epithet Ghorrat ol-'ayn (Solace of the eyes). These lines from one of her poems express the atmosphere of expectation in which the Bab's followers spent their days:

> The day of truth is here! Lies have turned to dust!
> Order, justice and law are now possible.
> Smashed, the despot's fist! God's hand opens:
> Grace pours down—not sorrow, pain and trouble . . .[4]

Having called for the abrogation of Islamic law and supported by some one hundred thousand devotees throughout Iran, the Bab posed an unprecedented threat to both Ghajar and clerical authority. Tahereh signaled the end of Islamic law by removing her veil during a conference of Babis at Badasht in northern Iran in 1848. Among those present at the conference was one Mirza Hossein Ali from the town of Nur on the Caspian coast. He later came to be known as Baha'u'llah, the founder of the Baha'i faith.

Mohammad Shah died in September of that year, triggering Babi uprisings throughout the country. Conservative Shi'ites, egged on by the clergy, responded by massacring Babis by the hundreds or even thousands. The Bab, Tahereh, and other Babi leaders were arrested, and most were executed in 1852. Baha'u'ullah survived by going underground, reemerging during the following decade as the voice of the newly pacifist Baha'is.

Mohammad Shah was succeeded upon his death in 1848 by his seventeen-year-old son Naser od-din, who was guided throughout the early years of his career by his prime minister and former tutor, Amir Kabir. Heralded by many as Iran's first modernist reformer, Amir Kabir's main concern was to centralize government power—an elusive prospect when most of the country remained in the hands of tribal warlords and feudal landowners.

Amir Kabir was largely responsible for crushing the Babi threat and ordering the execution of its leaders. Having previously gained experience as a representative of Iranian interests in Ottoman Turkey, he was impressed by the modernist reforms taking place there known as the *tanzimat*. He noticed particularly that the Sultan's ability to push through administrative and military changes had been made possible by reducing the political power of the Ottoman clergy.

Amir Kabir sought to improve the fortunes of the Ghajar state by exercising greater control over expenditures and more efficient tax collection from the provinces. In the field of agriculture he introduced cash crops such as cotton and sugarcane, and in medicine he launched a vaccination campaign against smallpox that saved many Iranian lives. He founded Iran's first modern institution of higher learning, the Dar ol-fonun (Institute of Technology), which would later evolve into Tehran University. The newspaper he established, *Vaghiye-ye-ettefaghiyeh* (Current Events), provided a window onto global affairs—at least for the small proportion of Iranians who could read.

Amir Kabir's aim to re-situate Iran within a rapidly changing world was reflected in his foreign policy as well. He was perhaps the first political leader in modern history to advocate a "non-aligned" approach, taking a firm stand against both British and Russian colonial maneuverings. At the same time, he cultivated relations with Iran's religious minority communities (except the Babis, who were considered to be merely Shi'ite heretics), recognizing the interest that European states had in their welfare. Not surprisingly given his growing power, British and Russian agents conspired with members of the royal family to have Amir Kabir removed from the scene. After just three years in office, he was assassinated while taking a bath in Kashan's Fin garden in January 1852.

Ghajar Iran was at the western edge of the buffer zone between the ever-expanding British and Russian empires in Asia and was considered too important for either power to allow the other to dominate. To the east it was a different story, with the Russians and the British both actively seeking to incorporate the lands of Central Asia into their respective empires. The Russians followed the eastward trajectory they had maintained since the sixteenth century, while the British attempted to penetrate from the opposite direction through Afghanistan.

The British military advance was thwarted on two occasions by the indomitable Pushtuns, a pair of disastrous adventures known as the First and Second Anglo-Afghan Wars which occurred in 1839–42 and 1878–81, respectively. Concurrent with the first engagement, two British agents, Colonel Charles Stoddart and Captain Arthur Conolly, were arrested in Bukhara. They were imprisoned under miserable conditions for three years before being executed as spies. As the Bukharan ruler, Abd us-Samad Khan, later explained to the English missionary Joseph Wolff, he had disliked the pride displayed by his English captives. The emir had reproached Conolly, saying, "You Englishmen come into a country in a stealthy manner, and take it." To this accusation, the latter unrepentingly replied, "We do not come in a stealthy manner; but we went openly and in daylight to Kabul, and took it."[5]

The Russians were more successful, seizing the Central Asian cities of Tashkent in 1865 and Samarkand in 1868, then forcing a severely truncated Emirate of Bukhara to accept the status of Russian protectorate five years later. Beginning in 1867, the Central Asian lands directly annexed by Russia were administered by the Turkestan Governate, which included most of present-day Kazakhstan as well as the Samarkand and Fergana Valley regions. The Russian conquests opened up Central Asia to colonization by large waves of Russian settlers, a process that continued into the twentieth century.

In Iran meanwhile, with Amir Kabir no longer on the scene, the young Naser od-din took an increasingly authoritarian approach to government. His attempt to recapture Herat in 1856 was halted by the British, forcing him to acknowledge their power in the region as well as the unalterable reality of the Afghan buffer state in lands that had historically belonged to Iran.

Naser od-din's failed Afghan campaign was also a disturbing sign of the Ghajar government's own fundamental weakness and inefficacy. They controlled the capital, Tehran, but for practical purposes most of the rest of the country was under the sway of corrupt local officials and restive tribesmen who did whatever they liked. Often as not, what they liked was raiding caravans, robbing travelers, and turning cropland into pasture, none of which was good for the national economy. As one visitor said of the Bakhtiari tribal region near Shiraz: "the women weave carpets, bags, and saddle-cloths, tend the flocks, and prepare the food of the men; the latter do little but plunder, except when the neighboring Persian princes require their services as soldiers."[6] In the northeastern part of the country, Turkmen bandits frequently captured villagers and carted them off to Central Asia to sell as slaves. In the absence of government protection, many of Iran's farmers abandoned agriculture and joined up with the nomads.

Apart from widespread lawlessness, Iran in the nineteenth century suffered from several serious epidemics of plague and cholera, followed by a severe famine in 1871 that caused well over a million deaths from starvation. Virtually the only medical facilities in the country were clinics run by European missionaries, who founded a number of modern schools as well. The missionary presence provided distinct advantages for Iran's religious minorities, who were less reluctant than Muslims to make use of their services.

Awakened to the dominant role now played in global affairs by the European powers (and perhaps wishing to escape from his responsibilities at home), Naser od-din Shah made three state visits to Europe, in 1873, 1878, and 1889. These trips were really grand, hugely expensive personal tours, which exhausted the Iranian state treasury. The American writer Mark Twain, reporting on the Shah's visit to London for the *New York Herald*, described him as a "splendid barbarian, who is lord over a few deserts and a modest ten million of ragamuffins . . . a man who has never done anything to win our gratitude or excite our admiration, except that he managed to starve a million of his subjects to death in twelve months."[7]

Naser od-din, on the other hand, was deeply impressed by what he saw in Europe during the course of these visits, particularly the crowds that thronged the streets. (His own capital of Tehran was still little more than a village at this point.) He was impressed by European wealth as well and sought to tap into it by offering attractive concessions to European businesses willing to invest in Iran.

Many Iranians saw these concessions as evidence that the shah was selling out the nation's resources to foreign interests, especially since the accompanying cash payments tended to go directly into the pocket of Naser od-din himself. The people weren't fooled, and popular opposition blocked his plan to hand over construction of Iran's railways

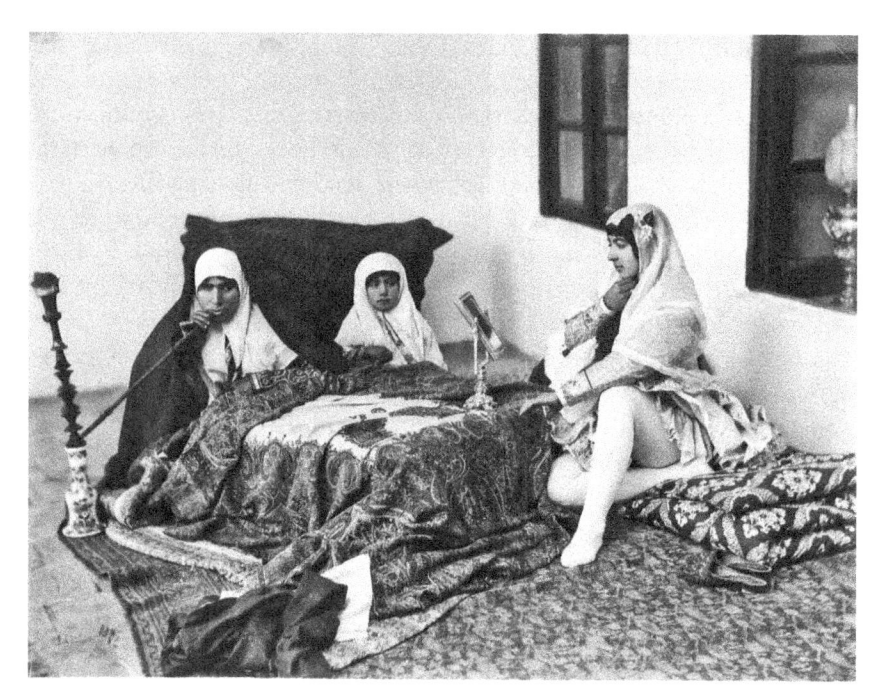

Royal Ghajar women and girl at leisure; the woman on the left smokes a qalyun (waterpipe), while the one on the right admires herself in a mirror. Ghajar women, many of whom spent lives of boredom sequestered within large harems, were renowned for their boldness and love of pleasures and became the source for many bawdy tales and songs still common today. Photo by Antoin Sevruguin, late nineteenth century, courtesy Brooklyn Museum 1997.4.3.

and canals to European firms. The bankrupt monarch did not give up, however.

Naser od-din's attempts to fill his personal coffers at the country's expense seriously backfired when he offered a monopoly on Iran's tobacco production to a British entrepreneur, Gerald F. Talbot. A leading cleric, Ayatollah Shirazi, issued a *fatwa* declaring the use of tobacco "un-Islamic" (*haram*), at least under the circumstances; virtually overnight an entire nation of nicotine addicts, men and women, quit the habit, forcing the shah to revoke his concession. The effectiveness of this "Tobacco Revolt" probably surprised all concerned and was an ominous foretaste of the power Iran's religious leaders could exercise over public behavior.

Widespread outrage at Naser od-din's wasteful and capitulatory policies found voice in the work of Mirza Malkom Khan, an Armenian Christian educated in Paris who converted to Islam as an adult. Malkom had been an instructor at the new Dar ol-fonun before entering the diplomatic service. His repeated calls for the rule of law to replace the unrestrained powers of the monarch put him in a tense relationship with Naser od-din Shah, and he was forcibly exiled on two occasions.

Nevertheless, it is said that the newpaper he published from London, *Qanun* (The Law), was personally read by the shah and his advisors. In a typical contribution, Malkom responds to the question, "What is unlawful government?" with the following definition: "That which plunders its subjects at will, sells the rights of the nation to any foreigner who wants them, wastes the kingdom's treasures on any base whim, shamelessly exploits the salaries and claims of its employees, brazenly denies its obligations and pacts, and plucks out your eyes whenever it pleases, throws your family in the street, confiscates your property, and slits your stomach open." To many Iranians, this description must have seemed all too familiar. But Malkom's solution is a simple one: "What should we do to change this? Become a human being and demand the Law."[8]

This is not to say that modern ideas were not taking Islamic forms as well. One of the most influential Islamic modernists of the nineteenth century, Jamal od-din "Afghani," claimed an Afghan identity to conceal his true origins, given that he spent most of his activist life in the Sunni world and advocated unity among all Muslims. He was in fact from an Iranian Shi'ite family, born in a village near Hamadan.

Jamal od-din's worldview was deeply marked by a visit to India that coincided with the failed "Indian Mutiny" (or "First War of Indian Independence") in 1857, which was brutally crushed by the British. He concluded that European imperialism was a danger that Muslim societies must resist at all costs, but at the same time, this resistance could only be achieved by these same Muslim societies modernizing themselves from within. Moving first to Ottoman Istanbul and later to Cairo, Jamal od-din became a staunch advocate of Muslims adopting Western educational methods, technologies, and political institutions, but in keeping with fundamental Islamic principles. There was, in his view, no inherent contradiction between "true" Islam and modern scientific rationality.

Jamal od-din's thought centered on the use of reason, and he blamed the backwardness of Muslims on their "imitation" (*taghlid*) of outdated precedents. In its broad outlines, this approach has characterized most Islamic reform movements of the twentieth century and into the present. Jamal od-din's views on *taghlid* are summed up in the following passage from one of his essays: "In their beliefs [the members of each community] must shun submission to conjectures and not be content with mere *taqlid* of their ancestors. For if man believes in things without proof or reason, makes a practice of following unproven opinions, and is satisfied to imitate and follow his ancestors, his mind inevitably desists from intellectual movement and little by little stupidity and imbecility overcome him."[9]

For Islamic modernists such as Jamal od-din who opposed blind imitation and mindless superstition, the Sufis were seen as the primary culprits. Even the classical poets so beloved by Iranians came under fire. In the words of another modernist, Mirza Agha Khan Kermani, "Their sonnets about roses and nightingales have encouraged the youth to pursue pederasty and booze."[10]

The shah himself was a selective fan of Western modernity. Apart from expensive trips to Europe, Naser od-din's private interests included poetry and the arts—not just painting and drawing, but also the new medium of photography. One of Iran's first professional photographers, the Armenian-Georgian Antoine Sevruguin, enjoyed the shah's patronage and produced many candid portraits of royal life. Naser od-din's forty-nine-year reign—the longest in three hundred years—was put to an end by an assassin's bullet in 1896. The hanging of his killer, a fanatic follower of Jamal od-din, was preserved in an eerie photograph by Sevruguin.

To his son and successor, Mozaffar od-din Shah, the profligate Naser od-din bequeathed a state in utter financial ruin. The new shah was forced to take out still further loans from Russia and Britain to finance Iran's debts. Needless to say, these sell-out measures severely compromised the country's political and economic sovereignty.

Mozaffar od-din also inherited his father's taste for European travel. During one of his tours he discovered cinema, a medium with which he became deeply enamored. Iran's film industry, which has garnered prizes at international festivals over the past several decades, owes its origins to Mozaffar od-din's enthusiastic support.

Two events marked Mozaffar od-din's reign that would have a major and lasting significance for Iran's development into a modern country. One was the so-called Constitutional Revolution beginning in 1905, whereby a broad coalition of disaffected Iranians including reformist intellectuals, bazaar merchants, and activist clerics took advantage of the government's weakness and unpopularity to push for significant political reforms. These included the establishment of Iran's first elected parliament, the Majles, which was formed in 1906, and creation of a formal constitution limiting royal powers.

Mozaffar od-din, who was ill and dying at this point, signed the new constitution on December 31 of the same year and passed away five days later.

The new shah, Mozaffar od-din's son Mohammad Ali, had opposed the constitution from the start. Once in power he immediately began trying to overturn it, by setting the different constitutionalist factions against each other and declaring the constitution itself contrary to Islamic law. He enlisted the support of his British and Russian creditors to close down the parliament, which was bombarded by a combination of Persian and Russian forces in June 1908. The British and Russians had signed an accord several months earlier dividing Iran into two spheres of influence, allotting the northern half of the country to the Russians and the southern half to the British.

The second game-changing event to occur during this period was connected to British designs on the south. In 1908, a team funded by English entrepreneur William Knox D'Arcy discovered oil at Masjed-e Solayman in southwestern Iran, seat of the great Elamite civilization in ancient times. The Anglo-Persian Oil Company (APOC)—forerunner to today's British Petroleum—was established the following year, with D'Arcy as its director. For the next five decades Iran's oil industry would be largely in the hands of British engineers and managers, along with a lion's share of its profits.

The struggles between pro- and anti-constitutionalist forces developed into something of a civil war that lasted through the end of World War I. The constitutionalists gained the upper hand in 1909, forcing Mohammad Ali into exile and replacing him with his son Ahmad. The new shah proved supportive of the parliament, but ineffective as a political leader.

Iran's fledgling constitutional monarchy had to contend with an ongoing financial crisis and continued interference from the Russians and the British, who used Iranian territory for proxy struggles against the Ottomans throughout the First World War. Bolshevik revolutionaries became active in northern Iran, while the British tried to consolidate their power over the oil-rich lands in the south. By 1919, when Ahmad Shah signed the Anglo-Persian Agreement granting Britain exclusive drilling rights throughout the country, Ghajar government control hardly extended beyond Tehran and its immediate surroundings. Thus, while Iran is virtually unique in the non-Western world in that it never formally became a colony of any European state, for practical purposes its autonomy had been sacrificed to British and Russian interests.

As in other, more directly colonized countries, some of Iran's art was sacrificed as well. Among the most distinctive artifacts from ancient Iran are bronze objects from the twelfth to seventh centuries BCE whose provenance is the region of Lorestan in the southern Zagros Mountains. The Lorestan Bronzes, as they are called, were mostly looted by locals from tombs beginning in the 1920s for sale on the European art market. They include such items as small human and animal figurines (some of which may have served as idols), jewelry, and military gear such as weapons and horse bits.

It fell to a highly charismatic and talented military officer from the Ghajars' Russian-trained Cossack Brigade, a certain Reza Khan from the town of Alasht in the northern province of Mazandaran, to organize a military coup and take over the reins of government in 1921. His first

This bronze horse bit from was made in Lorestan in the early first millennium BCE. The Lorestan bronzes are typically stylized human or animal figurines and were used to adorn weapons, horse harnesses, or jewelry such as pins and bracelets. Los Angeles County Museum of Art M.76.97.102

act was to send an army against the so-called Jangalis (forest-dwellers), an anti-landowner movement that had been active throughout the lush southwest Caspian province of Gilan since 1914.

With the support of the newly victorious Bolsheviks in Russia, the Jangalis had set up a "Persian Soviet Socialist Republic" in May 1920. Reza Khan's forces defeated the rebels in the summer of 1921. The border between Iran and the newly formed USSR was confirmed along the Araxes River, dividing the region of Azerbaijan into a Soviet Republic in the north and an Iranian province in the south. Reza Khan emerged as Iran's most powerful political figure, overshadowing the Ghajar king whose rule he was charged to defend.

CHAPTER 7

Modernization and Dictatorship: The Pahlavi Years (1925–1979)

Abandoned by his erstwhile Bolshevik supporters and on the run from Reza Khan's reinvigorated national army, Mirza Kuchik Khan, fugitive leader of the short-lived Persian Soviet Socialist Republic, took refuge in the Khalkhal Mountains of northwestern Iran accompanied by a German-Russian adventurer known only as Gauk. On December 2, 1921, the two revolutionaries succumbed to frostbite. Their frozen corpses were discovered by a local landowner, who decapitated Kuchik Khan and sent his head to Reza Khan in Tehran as a show of support for the new government.

Simultaneous with Kuchik Khan's Jangali uprising in the aftermath of World War I, a Kurdish chieftain named Simko Shikak managed to gain control of the region west of Lake Urmia near the Ottoman border. Iran's Kurdish region maintained its autonomy until 1922, when Reza Shah crushed the rebellion and drove Simko into exile.

Emboldened by his success against the Jangalis and the Kurds, Reza Khan spent the next several years putting down revolts by tribal warlords throughout the country and consolidating his own authority. By 1923 he had become powerful enough to forcibly exile the country's nominal ruler, Ahmad Shah, to Europe, leaving Reza free to assemble his own government cabinet. It soon became clear that he was now the functioning head of state, a fact confirmed in 1925 when the parliament formally deposed Ahmad and declared Reza to be the new shah of Iran. He took the dynastic name Pahlavi, an ancient term meaning "heroic" that consciously evoked Iran's pre-Islamic past.

Impressed by the modernizing changes brought about by Atatürk, founder of the neighboring Republic of Turkey during the 1920s,

Reza Shah attempted to follow the charismatic Turkish leader's strong-arm model in transforming Iran into a modern nation. In addition to crushing the power of the tribes by forcing them to settle in villages and take up agriculture, his agenda included suppressing the influence of the Shi'ite clergy; constructing Western-style schools, hospitals, law courts, banks, factories, and communications systems; and opening up the public sphere to women. In an effort to create a unified national identity—so as to thwart regional and ethnic separatist movements among the nomads and non-Persians who constituted half the country's population—he banned forms of traditional clothing and insisted on the use of Persian as the sole national language.

Most of these changes were instituted by force and were often met with strong resistance. Reza Shah's relationship with the clergy was particularly tense, especially following an incident in March 1928 when he entered a holy shrine in Ghom and beat a cleric who had protested the queen's removing her veil there the day before. The shah banned the veil altogether in 1936, thereby establishing it as an ongoing symbol of Iran's increasing social polarization. In response, some conservative men simply kept their wives at home and hired prostitutes to accompany them to public functions.

Nevertheless, Reza Shah's autocratic rule brooked no opposition, whether from religious figures or from his own handpicked parliament. When a group of bazaar merchants, conservative villagers, and clerics staged a mass demonstration at the shrine of the Eighth Imam in Mashhad in 1935, the shah sent in the army to disperse them, disregarding an age-old principle forbidding the violation of holy places. When his own government ministers disagreed with him he simply threw them in jail where they usually died, often under suspicious circumstances.

While he can be credited with catapulting Iran into the modern age in the space of little more than a decade, Reza Shah's achievements came at the cost of democracy and created social divisions that would haunt the country for years to come. He was, simply put, a military dictator, and in some ways his approach to running the nation resembled not so much Atatürk's as that of another of his contemporaries, Adolf Hitler, whom he frankly admired.

The prospect of increasing ties to Germany appealed to Reza Shah in several respects. Most important, it could act as a counterweight to the influence of Britain and the Soviet Union in Iranian affairs. There was a sentimental factor as well, however, which stemmed from Nazi

Germany's appropriation of Aryan ideology. Since the nineteenth century German scholars, recognizing that "Iran" literally means "Land of the Aryans," had been among Europe's most enthusiastic students of ancient Iranian history and languages. In 1935, acting on the advice of the Iranian ambassador to Berlin, Reza Shah decreed that henceforth "Persia" would be referred to as "Iran" within the world of diplomacy.

Naturally, this pro-German policy was not acceptable to either Britain or the Soviet Union, and after the two countries became allies against the Germans in 1941, they launched a joint invasion of Iran in August of that year. Reza Shah was deposed and exiled to South Africa, where he died of heart disease three years later. In his place the allies installed his inexperienced, Swiss-educated twenty-one-year-old son, Mohammad Reza Pahlavi.

While the changes brought about during Reza Shah's reign were dramatic, they did not affect Iranian society evenly across the board, and despite his attempts to unify the country and centralize government control his policies increased social divisions in many ways. The benefits of industrialization, improved education, and greater opportunities for women accrued disproportionately to the urban elites and the landowning class, at a time when a majority of the population remained landless, poor, and illiterate. Reza Shah's attempts to forcibly settle Iran's many nomadic tribes, most notably the Bakhtiaris, Ghashghais, Shahsevan, and Turkmen, only made them more antagonistic toward government authority.

The urban upper classes became increasingly Westernized during Reza Shah's reign, thanks to their increasing exposure to European goods and culture and the Western-style education they received at Iran's newly established universities or abroad. A secular intellectual class emerged that espoused democratic notions and applied Western models in the creation of literature and the arts.

Writers such as Mohammad Ali Jamalzadeh and Sadegh Hedayat had close connections to Europe. In fact, Jamalzadeh spent most of his long life in Geneva, and Hedayat ended his in Paris where he is buried. Hedayat's short existence was a tortured one—he committed suicide at the age of forty-eight—and this is apparent in his most successful novel, *The Blind Owl*. A nightmare vision of alienation and death, the book sets the tone from the very first sentence: "There are sores which slowly erode the mind in solitude like a kind of canker."[1]

Iran's first major modernist poet, Nima Yushij, was educated at a Catholic school in Tehran. He broke with Iran's centuries-old model of classical poetry with its rigid meters and limited stock of images, emphasizing instead impressions gained from nature:

> In the cold winter night
> Not even the hearth of the sun
> Burns like the hot hearth of my lamp
> And no lamp is as luminous as mine,
> Nor is frozen down the moon that shines above.[2]

With poetry so central to Iranians' sense of identity, Yushij's iconoclastic approach took time to win acceptance. Eventually, however, most Iranian poets followed his lead and embraced the chance to break free of the constraints of classical forms.

Ahmad Kasravi, born into a religious family, rejected his clerical upbringing and became modern Iran's best-known rationalist. He did not reject Shi'ite Islam per se, but his criticisms of its clerical class and many of its central beliefs were devastating. "So much has happened in the world," he notes, "which they [the clergy] have either not known or understood or have understood but have not paid any attention to. They live in the present, but cannot look at the world except from the perspective of thirteen hundred years ago."[3] Put on trial for blasphemy, the progressive-minded Kasravi was assassinated in court by a fanatical Islamist in 1946.

After installing Mohammad Reza on the Iranian throne in September 1941, the allied forces were able to use Iran to channel supplies to the USSR, their temporary ally of convenience, in an operation known as the "Persian Corridor." At the same time, the Soviet Union had plans of its own in dealing with its southern neighbor. Nationalist feeling had continued to simmer among the Kurds, in Iran as in other countries where they lived. The Soviets, following their occupation of northern Iran after Reza Shah's abdication, took advantage of this to set up a Kurdish puppet state. With military support from Iraqi Kurds led by Mustafa Barzani, it evolved into the Republic of Mahabad as the war ended in 1945. Another Soviet-sponsored entity was created in Iranian Azerbaijan at the same time, playing on Azeri nationalist sentiment.

Soviet forces withdrew from the region the following year, however, and the two fledgling states were forcibly reincorporated into Iran. The Kurdish language was officially banned, and the "president" of the Mahabad Republic, Ghazi Mohammad, was executed for treason. Barzani, who had been elected in absentia to head the new Kurdish Democratic Party (KDP) in Iraq, fled instead to the

Soviet Union, where he remained until 1958. These failed Soviet adventures in Iranian territory fueled an emerging Cold War paranoia that would serve as justification for Western interference over the years to come.

During the early postwar period young Mohammad Reza initially showed himself to be more cautious and more accommodating than his father, both at home and abroad. His attitude toward the clergy was markedly more open, while the educated classes, freed from the iron-fisted rule of Reza Shah, began to agitate for a more functional parliamentary democracy.

The communist Tudeh party grew in popularity, particularly among the increasingly literate underclasses who were becoming more politicized. A women's branch of the party was founded by Maryam Farman-Farmayan, a Ghajar princess, saying that the Tudeh were the only party in Iran who would take a feminist like herself. "Red Mary," as she was known, hosted gatherings of intellectuals in the Parisian salon tradition; the writer Sadegh Hedayat was a frequent guest.

By the end of the decade, nationalist sentiment was largely focused on obtaining a higher share of Iran's oil profits, which were controlled by the British-owned Anglo-Iranian Oil Company (AIOC). In March 1951, after failing to reach an agreement with AIOC, the Iranian parliament voted to nationalize the oil industry. Six weeks later a newly appointed prime minister, Mohammad Mossadegh, carried out the nationalization. In response, an outraged Great Britain did everything in its power to prevent Iran from selling its oil, while simultaneously conducting covert operations within the country aimed at undermining Mossadegh's efforts.

The Iranian prime minister initially hoped to gain support from the supposedly pro-democracy United States, but the British thwarted this by opportunistically playing up US fears of a communist takeover in Iran. Given Iran's long-standing dislike of Russia, this was never a real possibility, but Britain managed to turn the US administration against Mossadegh nevertheless. British intelligence then enlisted the fledgling American Central Intelligence Agency (CIA) to organize a coup d'état, which took place in August 1953. Mossadegh was placed under house arrest and the pro-shah army general Fazlollah Zahedi, who had carried out the coup using CIA funds and hired street gangs, was made prime minister. Western media praised Iran for "preventing a potential communist takeover," while the CIA quietly congratulated itself on having carried out its first successful "regime change" operation.

Mohammad Mossadegh, prime minister of Iran's first democratically elected government which nationalized Iran's oil industry, met with US President Harry S. Truman in Washington, DC, in October 1951. Although Mossadegh initially hoped the United States would support his democratically elected regime, he was toppled by a CIA-led coup in 1953, an act that has continued to symbolize Western hypocrisy in the minds of many Iranians. National Park Service photo by Abbie Rowe, courtesy Harry S. Truman Presidential Library and Museum, accession number 73-3803

The 1953 coup established the United States as a major player in the Middle East, with Iran as its principal ally. US influence in Iran took conflicting forms. On the one hand, the Americans supported a number of economic and social changes, including breaking up feudal estates, increasing industrialization, and giving women the right to vote. At the same time, fearing threats to the shah's power, the CIA created a secret police force, called the SAVAK, which would terrorize the Iranian population for the next two decades.

The equation of "modernity" with "Westernness" had been criticized as early as the second half of the nineteenth century by Jamal od-din "Afghani" and others. By the 1950s the rapid pace of change, especially in major cities such as Tehran, seemed to many Iranians to represent an unquestioning capitulation to Western superiority. Perhaps the most vocal critic of elite Iranians' infatuation with the West was the writer Jalal Al-e Ahmad, author of the groundbreaking 1962 book *Gharbzadegi* (West-struckness). Al-e Ahmad saw Western culture as a disease that was ravaging Iranians from within: "I could say that *gharbzadegi* is like cholera. If this seems distasteful I could say it's like heatstroke or frostbite. But no. It is at least as bad as sawflies in the wheat fields. Have you ever seen how they infest wheat? From within. There is a healthy skin in place, but it is only a skin, just like the shell of a cicada on a tree. In any case, we're talking about a disease."[4]

Al-e Ahmad's style was demagogical and not particularly literary, but it resonated with many Iranians. He was better at offering criticisms than solutions, however. In seeking to identify "authentic" Iranianness he settled on Shi'ism, but his own Shi'ite identity ultimately eluded him. This frustration is evident in the account he wrote of his pilgrimage to Mecca, tellingly entitled *Lost in the Crowd*.

In 1963, the shah launched a series of reforms he called the "White Revolution." Perhaps the most significant of these reforms was a land redistribution scheme whereby the government bought up land from wealthy landlords and resold it at a discount to the peasants who farmed it. As a vehicle for redistributing wealth, this program failed, since the resulting plots of land were so small that the peasants often ended up simply selling them back to the former owners. The landed aristocracy, for their part, complained bitterly, even as they benefited from opportunities to buy factories in or near major cities and to mechanize agricultural production in the countryside. Peasants whose labor was no longer needed on the farms flocked to the cities in search of factory work; most wound up unemployed, uprooted, and living in urban slums.

A more openly controversial aspect of the shah's reforms was the establishment of women's suffrage in 1963. This controversy was largely symbolic since Iran's elections were not particularly democratic, but religious conservatives saw it as an unacceptable precedent and raised an outcry. Many of the protesters were students in the seminary city of Ghom. The shah's strong-armed response to these protests was roundly condemned by a fearless cleric named Ruhollah Khomeini.

The clergy as a whole were not happy with the changes brought about by the shah—many of them came from landowning families that resented the breaking up of estates—but traditional Shi'ite quietism, which resignedly held that all governments until the return of the Twelfth Imam are illegitimate, combined with fear of the secret police, prevented them from speaking up. "Ayatollah" Khomeini, meanwhile—the title, accorded to high-ranking clerics, means "Sign of God"—won the admiration of many rank-and-file Iranians for his willingness to speak out against the shah. Not surprisingly, in June 1963 he was arrested, sparking demonstrations during which government forces killed several hundred protestors. In what was likely a protective move, Khomeini's colleagues quickly elevated him to the supreme clerical rank of *Marja' ot-taghlid* (Source of Emulation), which preserved him from any punishment beyond house arrest.

The following year the shah attempted to rid himself of further trouble by sending Khomeini into exile, first to Turkey and then to the holy Shi'ite city of Najaf in Iraq. This decision proved to have the opposite effect from what was intended, however, since Khomeini was then free to denounce the shah's policies from a safe distance outside the country. This he did for the next fourteen years, with catastrophic consequences for the shah.

A highly emotional target for criticism was the shah's extension of diplomatic immunity to all Americans living in Iran, an expatriate community that exceeded fifty thousand at its peak. Khomeini caustically remarked in one of his speeches that "If an Iranian runs over an American's dog he will face prosecution . . . but if an American cook runs over the shah [himself], no one can do anything."[5]

For many Iranians, an even greater demonstration of the shah's disregard for his own people was an enormously extravagant and astronomically expensive event he organized at Persepolis in 1971, celebrating "two thousand five hundred years of Iranian monarchy." He invited royalty and heads of state from around the world, though most chose not to attend. During the course of this ostentatious self-congratulatory exercise, the shah earned widespread ridicule by standing before the tomb of Cyrus the Great at nearby Pasargadae and pompously proclaiming, "Sleep well, Cyrus, for We are awake." Foreign guests traveling to and from Persepolis could not fail to notice the grinding poverty of the villages along the way.

Radicalism, so widespread in the 1960s, also found expression in Iran, not only among the intelligentsia but in the arts as well. A number of young filmmakers, many of them influenced by French New Wave directors such as Jean-Luc Godard and François Truffaut, broke the commercial mold of popular violence-and-betrayal type movies (derisively called *film farsi*) and explored more avant-garde forms of cinema. A prime example is Dariush Mehrjui's surrealistic film *The Cow* (1969), in which a destitute farmer is so distraught by the death of his cow that he takes on the role of a cow himself.

In the field of literature, Iranian poets and novelists continued to explore new styles. Ahmad Shamlu drew inspiration from both classical poets and modernists such as Nima Yushij, as well as from French literature and even Japanese haiku. Sohrab Sepehri explored Buddhist culture and was also an accomplished painter. The novelist Hushang Golshiri was known for his dense prose and subtle allegory; Iran's most prestigious literary award is named for him.

Forugh Farrokhzad was the first Iranian poet to express herself as an independent, sexual woman:

> Desire surged in his eyes
> red wine swirled in the cup
> my body surfed all over his
> in the softness of the downy bed.[6]

Her work drew controversy, and after spending a number of years living unapologetically as the mistress of filmmaker Ebrahim Golestan, Farrokhzad died at the age of thirty-two in a suspicious car accident. "Forugh," as she is affectionately called by her many admirers, remains an iconic figure for Iranian feminists. Another highly respected woman poet, Simin Behbahani, also won international acclaim, being twice nominated for the Nobel Prize in Literature.

Shah Mohammad Reza's first two marriages failed to produce an heir, but his third wife, Farah Diba, bore a son, Reza, in October 1960, a mere ten months after wedding the shah. When her royal husband decided to hold a lavish coronation ceremony for himself in 1967 (twenty-six years into his reign), taking the grandiose title "Light of the Aryans," he added to the occasion by crowning Farah as empress. In the years that followed, Farah was given wide-ranging responsibilities, not only in government but also as head of numerous humanitarian and artistic enterprises.

Mohammad Reza Pahlavi, the last shah of Iran, with his wife Farah Diba at Andrews Air Force Base during a trip to the United States in November 1977. The shah, a staunch US ally who attempted to modernize Iran even as he struggled to maintain absolutist control, was toppled by a popular revolution in 1979, bringing an end to two thousand five hundred years of Iranian monarchy. US Air Force MSgt. Denham / Department of Defense Visual Information Center

Farah's work in health and education projects took her to cities and villages all over Iran, giving her a better sense of the country's realities than that possessed by the shah. The public did not fail to notice the difference, and the empress was arguably much more popular than the shah himself. Her involvement in the arts, meanwhile, which included purchasing many works by well-known artists from all over the world, made her a known and respected figure on the international art scene. Her chief artistic advisor was the painter Aydin Aghdashlu—himself a master of Renaissance, classical Persian, and magical realist styles—who acquired works by Monet, Picasso, Warhol, and other Western artists on behalf of the empress.

In 1973 an event occurred that dramatically altered Iran's economy. As a protest against Western support for Israel in the Yom Kippur War against Egypt and Syria, the oil cartel known as the Organization of Petroleum Exporting Countries (OPEC)—which was under the shah's leadership at the time—declared an embargo on oil sales to the West. The price of oil increased fourfold almost overnight. This produced a severe economic crisis in countries such as the United States that had grown dependent on cheap oil and created a windfall for oil-producing countries like Iran.

Iran's massive oil wealth made possible advances in the fields of industry, education, and public health. Women and religious minorities—including Baha'is, Jews, and Christians who had early on embraced Western forms of education—saw increased access to education and jobs. Ultimately, however, the surge in riches benefited mainly the elite urban classes, especially those with connections to the royal family. Ordinary consumers, meanwhile, were hit hard by unchecked inflation. The bazaars were flooded with foreign goods, at prices domestic producers could not compete with. Iranian farmers in particular were devastated by cheap imports of food staples such as wheat.

Nor were these social and economic changes accompanied by increased political freedoms. As growing numbers of people entered the educated classes and became more politically aware, rising expectations for greater public participation in governance could not be met within Iran's totalitarian system. Two officially sanctioned political parties were meant to provide a semblance of democracy, but since both parties were ultimately answerable to the shah they were dismissively referred to as the "Yes, Your Majesty Party" and the "Yes, *certainly*, Your Majesty Party." Eventually the shah dispensed with this charade and in 1975 created a single political party, called Rastakhiz (Resurgence), which people were forced to join. Rather than increasing his support base as intended, this move had the opposite effect of negatively politicizing many individuals who had previously been apolitical.

Much of the money generated by Iran's oil industry was used to buy expensive military equipment from the United States or disappeared into the pockets of the shah's cronies. Even as Iran's urban elites were amassing fortunes, massive rural displacements due to the mechanization of agriculture created a burgeoning urban underclass. This included large numbers of unemployed single men who had little to do but while away their days hanging around in neighborhood mosques where they could find a sense of community and share their complaints. Often their entertainment would consist of sitting together and listening to inflammatory speeches by Khomeini, smuggled into the country on cassette tapes from Iraq.

Within Iran, a dissident form of Shi'ism was promoted by Ali Shari'ati, a sociologist trained in Paris. As a student, Shari'ati had been friends with members of the Algerian Liberation Front (a radical organization fighting to throw off French colonial rule), and he was deeply influenced by Frantz Fanon's anti-colonial tract *The Wretched of the Earth*, which Shari'ati translated into Persian. During the 1960s and 1970s he lectured at an institute in Tehran known as the Hosseiniyeh Ershad, where he was highly popular among progressive-minded religious students.

Shari'ati coined the term "red Shi'ism" (a reference to martyrs' blood, not to socialism) in opposition to the "black Shi'ism" of the clergy. In making this distinction he harkened back to the revolutionary example of the ill-fated Sarbedar sect in the fourteenth century: "for the first time, a revolutionary movement based on Alavite Shi'ism, against foreign domination, internal deceit, the power of the feudal lords and wealthy capitalists, had an armed uprising, led by peasants seven hundred years ago, under the banner of justice and the culture of martyrdom, for the salvation of the enslaved nation and the deprived masses."[7] Shari'ati's activism led to his arrest in 1974. After a year and a half he was released. In 1977 he left for England, but died three weeks later under suspicious circumstances.

The shah's heavy-handed rule also fostered the emergence of two militant leftist revolutionary groups, the religiously oriented Mojahedin-e Khalgh (MEK) and the Marxist Fedayin-e Khalgh. Both organizations staged attacks during the 1970s that were met with brutally repressive measures, including mass arrests, secret kidnappings, and a number of executions. The leftist threat provided the SAVAK secret police with a pretext to increase their harassment of ordinary citizens, further alienating the shah from the general population.

During the mid-1970s the shah developed cancer, which he kept secret from the public. As his condition worsened he began to make a series of misjudgments, ultimately leading to the revolution that ended his reign. Yet on a state visit to Tehran in December 1977, US president Jimmy Carter praised his host by declaring that "Iran, because of the great leadership of the Shah, is an island of stability in one of the more troubled areas of the world."[8] Events would soon demonstrate just how badly Carter had misread the situation.

Late 1977 had already seen several large public demonstrations against the shah's rule. Middle-class opposition groups such as the National Front—a remnant of Mossadegh's party—and the religious but moderate Freedom Movement of Iran (FMI) were growing stronger and better organized. The shah's government provoked religious hardliners, meanwhile, with an anonymous article in an official newspaper insulting the character of Ayatollah Khomeini. This led to riots in Ghom, resulting in a number of deaths. Another leading cleric, Ayatollah

Shari'atmadari, broke with the clergy's traditional quietest stance and joined the opposition.

The Ghom killings initiated a cycle of demonstrations every forty days—the traditional mourning period in Shi'ite Islam—in which both religious and secular protesters participated. Each time a few more individuals were killed by anti-riot forces, exacerbating public anger against the regime. The situation calmed somewhat in the summer of 1978 when the shah announced a number of reforms, including the ending of censorship and the promise of full democratic elections the following year. But a terrorist attack on a cinema in the southern city of Abadan on August 19, which some blamed on Islamists and others on the secret police, reignited tensions. As a result of a fire (which was later shown to have been set by an Islamic militant), 422 people died of flames or smoke inhalation when the doors to the cinema were locked from the outside.

Massive protests followed. At the same time, the shah began to make a number of concessions, including the legalization of political parties, the freeing of political prisoners, and the closing of nightclubs and casinos. These gestures, rather than appeasing the opposition, emboldened it. Street protests continued, drawing hundreds of thousands of protesters, which led the shah to declare martial law on September 8, 1978. That same day the army fired into a crowd of peaceful protesters, killing sixty-four unarmed civilians—an event that came to be remembered as Black Friday.

Ayatollah Khomeini, still in Iraq, capitalized on the public's growing outrage by making ever more incendiary speeches. At the suggestion of his advisors, Khomeini relocated to suburban Paris, where he enjoyed better access to advanced communications for the dissemination of his diatribes against the shah's regime. His messages found a widening audience among leftist and even secular members of the opposition, as well as some Western intellectuals such as the French philosopher Michel Foucault. Across Iran, a succession of workers' strikes throughout the autumn brought the country's economy to a virtual standstill.

Renewed street demonstrations in November led to anarchy, as the shah urged the security forces to exercise restraint. On December 2, an estimated two million protesters filled Tehran's Freedom Square on the occasion of 'Ashura commemorating the death of Imam Husayn—the young, handsome, virtuous grandson of the Prophet Muhammad who was killed in battle in 680 CE. Four days later the shah himself went on television and told the nation "I have heard the voice of your revolution." He apologized for his mistakes and promised to work with opposition parties to restore public order.

Nevertheless, protests in the following days brought millions more demonstrators into the streets all over the country. The shah responded by appointing a member of the opposition, National Front leader Shapur Bakhtiar, to the post of prime minister. It was too little too late. In the face of continuing unrest, the shah, now seriously ill with cancer, left the country on January 16, 1979, never to return.

With most countries unwilling to receive him, the shah wandered like the Flying Dutchman from Egypt to Morocco to the Bahamas and Mexico, before finally being admitted to the United States for medical treatment. Rather than give in to the demands of Iran's new revolutionary government that the shah be extradited home to face trial, the United States sent him on to Panama. After a short stay there, he returned to Egypt, where his cancer finally claimed him on July 27, 1980. The Pahlavi dynasty—along with Iran's tradition of monarchy stretching back more than twenty-five centuries—was at an end.

CHAPTER 8

The Islamic Republic of Iran (1979–present)

On February 1, 1979, a specially chartered Air France 747 left Paris for Tehran. On board were the Ayatollah Khomeini and a group of advisors, accompanied by one hundred twenty journalists. Asked by American news correspondent Peter Jennings what his feelings were on returning home after a fourteen-year exile, Khomeini dismissively replied, "Nothing."

For most of the others on board, the dominant emotion was fear: the Iranian military had given no assurances that it would not shoot down the plane as soon as it crossed into Iranian airspace. As it happened, they did not do so. The flight landed safely at Tehran's Mehrabad airport, where several million supporters welcomed Khomeini and his entourage. Newspaper headlines reinforced the popular hysteria with the inflammatory headline, "The Imam Has Come," playing up messianic expectations latent in the collective psychology of the largely Shi'ite nation.

Iranians from across the political spectrum—Marxist, secular democratic, and religious—had worked together to expel the shah. Among all the various revolutionary voices, however, only the charismatic religious leader Khomeini was able to inspire a mass following. Taking advantage of his broad grassroots support, Khomeini wasted no time in dismissing the fragile Bakhtiar government appointed by the departing shah, replacing it with a provisional administration led by the head of the Freedom Movement of Iran (FMI), a politically moderate engineer by the name of Mehdi Bazargan.

Faced with widespread public disorder in the major cities as well as separatist rebellions in several provinces, the new government created its own military body called the Pasdaran-e enghalab-e eslami, or Islamic Revolution Guard Corps (IRGC), in order to stave off any perceived threats to the revolution. Since then Iran has had essentially

Ayatollah Ruhollah Khomeini, Iran's exiled religious leader, emerges from an Air France plane after his arrival at Mehrabad Airport in Tehran, on February 1, 1979. Along with a retinue of family, aides, and journalists, he returned from Paris after fourteen years in exile. Associated Press/FY 7902010797

two armed forces: the traditional military, ostensibly responsible for fighting wars abroad, and the Revolutionary Guards, for maintaining internal security. Over time, the roles of the two became increasingly blurred.

In late March 1979 the provisional government held a national referendum, asking voters in simple terms whether or not they approved the establishment of an as yet undefined "Islamic Republic." Many boycotted the referendum, objecting to this lack of specificity, but among those who voted almost all were in favor. A republic was, after all, what most Iranians had been hoping for, and since 99 percent of Iranians were Muslim, it stood to reason that the new state would be "Islamic"—although most voters seem to have had little notion at the time of what this would prove to entail.

A new constitution drafted that summer offered some initial clues. The document provided for an elected parliament, but with ultimate power reserved for Khomeini. This was in keeping with his own unique theory of *velayat-e faghih*, or "Guardianship of the [Supreme] Jurist"—the principle that the head of government should be the person most qualified in Shi'ite jurisprudence. Khomeini had earlier written in a treatise on Islamic government (which few ordinary Iranians had read), "Since Islamic government is a government of law, those acquainted with the law, or more precisely, with religion—that is, the *foghaha*—must supervise its functioning. It is they who supervise all executive and administrative affairs of the country, together with all planning."[1] The unelected nature of the post of *faghih*, which was tailor-made for Khomeini himself and did not clearly specify a procedure for succession, imposed a constitutionally embedded limit on how far the democratic process in Iran could evolve in the years to come.

While the revolutionary government struggled to find its bearings, civil disorder prevailed throughout the country. Ad hoc neighborhood patrols—called *komiteh*s—broke into homes in search of alcohol and other items forbidden under Islamic law. These same unaccountable vigilante groups busily rounded up opposition figures and individuals with real or suspected ties to the former regime, many of whom were executed after kangaroo trials.

Following the admission of the shah to the United States for medical treatment in late October 1979, on November 4 a band of radical students stormed the US embassy in Tehran and took fifty-two US diplomats hostage. The hostages would not be released until 444 days later, after the swearing in of Ronald Reagan as US president in January 1981. This "hostage crisis" caused a permanent rift in Iran-US relations, with successive governments in each of the two countries casting the other as the quintessential enemy and source of evil in the world. The United States was labeled "the Great Satan," and Iranians were encouraged to tread on American flags painted on the ground.

The hostage crisis, which had resulted from a violation of the US embassy grounds in contravention to international law, led Iranian Prime Minister Bazargan to resign in disgust. Bazargan later expressed his dismay at the ongoing course of Iran's revolution in an open letter to parliament in 1982: "The government has created an atmosphere of terror, fear, revenge and national disintegration. . . . What has the ruling elite done in nearly four years, besides bringing death and destruction, packing the prisons and the cemeteries in every city, creating long queues, shortages, high prices, unemployment, poverty, homeless people, repetitive slogans and a dark future?"[2]

The Islamic Republic elected its first president, Abo'l-Hasan Bani Sadr, in January 1980. Prior to the election, Khomeini had banned most of the country's political parties. The only exceptions were the Islamic Republic Party (IRP—a party he himself had formed), Bazargan's FMI, and the leftist Tudeh and Feda'i parties. Khomeini would soon enough set his sights on eliminating the leftist parties as well.

Khomeini first denounced the Mojahedin-e Khalgh (MEK), an ostensibly Islamic group that had supported him throughout the revolution. Vigilante gangs of *hezbollahi*s (partisans of God) viciously attacked MEK members at their meeting sites and made a practice of harassing any other perceived opponents of Islamic rule. The *hezbollahi*s hounded Iran's religious minorities as well, especially Baha'is, whose entire leadership was arrested and presumably executed in secret. Although the new constitution recognized Iran's Christian, Jewish, and Zoroastrian communities, even guaranteeing them seats in parliament, Baha'is were excluded as an "illegal political faction"—a status they still retain.

One of Ayatollah Khomeini's stated aims was to export Iran's Islamic revolution, starting with countries that had large Shi'ite populations. In accordance with this policy Iran lent its support to the Hizbullah (Party of God) movement in southern Lebanon, which had been formed out of existing Shi'ite militias in response to Israel's 1982 invasion of that war-torn country. Close relations with the Lebanese Hizbullah over the subsequent decades would become a principal reason for the US government to classify Iran as a state sponsor of terrorism.

Another obvious target for Shi'ite revolution was Iraq, the country where Khomeini had spent most of his fourteen-year exile. In response to this threat, and employing the pretext of a long-standing border dispute, Iraqi president Saddam Hussein ordered the invasion of Iran on September 22, 1980. He clearly hoped to take advantage of Iran's internal problems, but the Iraqi invasion only served to strengthen the Iranian regime, galvanizing public support and providing justification for the merciless suppression of internal opposition. Apart from the regular army and the Revolutionary Guards, many young men and boys joined (or were forced to join) a volunteer fighting force called the Basij that would go on to thrive as a pro-government paramilitary force after the war.

The now underground MEK, meanwhile, saw the Iraq conflict as an opportunity to attack the Iranian regime from within. During the summer of 1981 they staged a series of bombings in which dozens of senior Iranian political figures were killed, including the president, the prime minister, and the chief justice. Khomeini's future successor as Supreme Leader, Ali Khamene'i, was also wounded in one of these attacks. The government responded by clamping down even harder on suspected MEK members, executing hundreds.

Throughout the eight-year war with Iraq, ordinary Iranians were subjected to extreme hardships. A generation of young men were sent to the war front, where more than six hundred thousand were killed and many more seriously wounded. Food staples were rationed, and many in Tehran and other cities lived under the daily threat of bombardments and blackouts.

In 1986, the Iran-Contra Affair erupted, resulting in a scandal that embarrassed both the US and Iranian governments. It was discovered that the two had been engaged in secret negotiations in which the United States agreed sell arms to Iran in violation of its own self-imposed embargo. In return, Iran would help free American hostages being held in Lebanon. The Reagan administration planned to use money received from Iran to covertly fund anti-government rebels in socialist Nicaragua, an act the US Congress had forbidden. Public outrage at these illegal goings-on erupted in both Iran and the United States, but the government culprits on both sides eventually emerged unscathed.

In the wake of this fiasco, the United States began more openly to support Iraq in its war against Iran, providing military intelligence and putting American flags on Kuwaiti oil tankers that were supplying Iraq to discourage Iran from attacking them. The MEK, now based in Iraq and collaborating with Saddam's regime, attempted to invade western Iran but were halted by Iranian forces. Most Iranians, regardless of their views concerning their own government, have seen the MEK as traitors ever since.

The Iran-Iraq war was finally concluded in 1988 without any permanent gains on either side, and Khomeini died the following year. Shortly before Khomeini's death, his anticipated successor Ayatollah Hossein Ali Montazeri distanced himself from the Supreme Leader by pointing out the government's record of political arrests and executions: "The denial of people's rights, injustice and disregard for the revolution's true values have delivered the most severe blows against the revolution. Before any reconstruction, there must first be a political and ideological reconstruction."[3] An outraged Khomeini responded by quickly ousting Montazeri and appointing Ayatollah Ali Khamene'i as his next-in-line.

Another of Khomeini's significant final gestures was to issue a *fatwa* (a formal legal opinion) to the effect that British writer Salman Rushdie, born a Muslim in British India, had apostatized from Islam—a ruling based on the allegedly blasphemous nature of Rushdie's book *The Satanic Verses* (which Khomeini himself had not read)—and was therefore liable to the death penalty under Islamic law. Khomeini's pronouncement led to massive demonstrations throughout the Muslim world and beyond, and a number of people, including several connected with the publishing industry, were killed. Rushdie himself went into hiding and made only rare public appearances thereafter. The United Kingdom suspended diplomatic relations with Iran from 1989 to 1998 over the Rushdie affair.

Iran's internal politics throughout that decade were dominated by the policies of President Ali Akbar Hashemi Rafsanjani, a cleric with strong ties to Iran's powerful merchant class. Rafsanjani was a conservative pragmatist who focused on rebuilding Iran's shattered economy while keeping a tight rein on social restrictions. Although Rafsanjani initiated a number of free market reforms, economic growth during this period was disappointing, especially after the imposition of US-led international sanctions in 1995.

Meanwhile Rafsanjani's daughter, Faezeh Hashemi, launched a political career of her own, serving in parliament from 1996 to 2000 and staying active in women's issues thereafter. Protected to some extent by her father's position, Hashemi created controversy by wearing jeans and encouraging women's sports, eventually founding a feminist newspaper. As she said in an interview, "Some customs in our society have been imposed, and an imposed custom is without value and cannot persist. Therefore, when I do not believe in certain customs and I do not believe them to be logical or I do not value them as beneficial to society, especially to girls and women, I do not see it necessary to follow them."[4]

A hugely successful family planning campaign established in 1989 brought Iran's pre-revolution fertility rate of six children per woman down to 1.71 by 2007. (Iran's population nevertheless doubled during this same period, from fewer than thirty-five million to more than seventy million, due to decreases in infant mortality and rising life expectancy.) Women's health clinics throughout the country provided sex education and contraceptives to all married couples, earning Iran the honor of having one of the best systems for women's reproductive rights in the world. Unfortunately, these progressive policies were eventually reversed.

The postwar decades also saw improvements in women's access to higher education and the workplace, although they were prevented from serving as judges due to a persistent stereotype questioning women's capacity to be impartial. Female university students came to outnumber males, and literacy reached even the remotest villages. Iranian women continued to face challenges in such areas as divorce and child custody laws, but women's rights activists made progress in these areas as well. In 2003 the Nobel Peace Prize was awarded to Iranian lawyer Shirin Ebadi, founder of Iran's Center for the Defense of Human Rights. This gesture served as an international acknowledgment of the diligence with which Iranian women were fighting for their rights in the face of a highly patriarchal regime. In Ebadi's view, "it is not religion that binds women, but the selective dictates of those who wish them cloistered."[5]

During the first decade of the revolution many of the intellectuals who had originally supported the Islamic Republic began to express disappointment with the way it was developing. Philosopher Abdolkarim Soroush was the most prominent among this group. Western journalists heralded him as an Islamic Martin Luther, but repeated harassment from government-supported thugs forced Soroush to leave Iran in 2000 and his thought had little impact thereafter. He remained popular within Western academia, however, receiving invitations to lecture at a number of prestigious institutions including Harvard, Yale, Princeton, Columbia, and the University of Chicago.

Another highly visible figure within the "loyal opposition" was Mohsen Kadivar, a cleric and philosophy teacher. Kadivar notably criticized Khomeini's principle of "Guardianship of the Jurist," arguing that it had no basis in Shi'ite thought. "It is time for the Supreme Leader to be subject to the constitution too," Kadivar wrote. "After all, the Supreme Leader doesn't come from God!"[6] Eventually, like Soroush, Kadivar left Iran to pursue a series of visiting teaching appointments in the United States.

The 1990s saw Iranian cinema garnering attention as one of the world's most dynamic and creative film industries, beginning with *The White Balloon* by Jafar Panahi—a touching story told from the perspective of children—which won the Golden Camera award at the Cannes Film Festival in 1995. Two years later *The White Balloon*'s scriptwriter, Abbas Kiarostami, won Cannes's most prestigious prize, the Golden Palm, for his film *A Taste of Cherry*. Kiarostami had been known for making films featuring children as a way of dealing with censorship, but this time his subject was suicide. In 2012, Asghar

Farhadi's film *A Separation* addressed another social taboo, showing the unbearable pressures brought by modern Iranian society on a young married couple. That year the film won Hollywood's Oscar for Best Foreign Film, introducing Iranian cinema to a mainstream American audience.

The temporary loosening of censorship during the 1990s and after came largely from the efforts of moderate cleric Mohammad Khatami, who served as minister of culture from 1982 to 1992. His surprise election as president in 1997, followed by that of a large number of reformists to parliament in 2000, led to significant changes in Iran's social and political climate, including a relaxation of social controls and a more open attitude toward the West. Khatami, well versed in Western philosophy, promoted the notion of Dialogue Among Civilizations—a clear rejoinder to Harvard political scientist Samuel Huntington's pessimistic "Clash of Civilizations" theory. He was equally direct in challenging intolerance within his own society. "If, God forbid," he wrote in a typical essay, "some people want to impose their rigid thinking on Islam and call it God's religion—since they lack the intellectual power to confront the opposite side's thinking on its own terms—they resort to fanaticism. This merely harms Islam, without achieving the aims of the people."[7]

Under Khatami's presidency independent newspapers began to flourish, modern art galleries thrived, and trendy cafés proliferated, while novels and films explored controversial subjects such as prostitution, government corruption, and drug abuse. Repressive measures against Baha'is were relaxed, allowing them to register their marriages and conduct funerals. Iran became second only to Sweden as a destination for sex-change operations, which Khomeini had authorized as preferable to homosexuality.

Enforcement of women's dress codes was eased, though not eliminated: fashionable urban girls pushed the limits of *hejab* by showing tufts of highlighted hair under flimsy headscarves and wearing tight-fitting *manteaux* in place of the chador. Nose jobs became so popular that wearing a bandage across one's septum became a fashion statement. Khatami appointed Iran's first female vice president, American-educated environmental activist Massumeh Ebtekar—a woman who, years earlier during the revolution, had acted as fiery spokesperson for the student hostage-takers at the US embassy.

The scope of Khatami's reforms was limited by opposition from hardline conservatives, many of whom held unelected positions in Iran's judiciary and security forces and were ultimately answerable to

Nose-job, *a 2005 painting by the Tehran-based woman artist Shohreh Mehran, evokes the massive popularity among young Iranian women for cosmetic rhinoplasty. In Iran today, where dress codes have forced women to find creative ways of expressing stylishness, wearing a nose bandage suggestive of surgery is seen as a status symbol.* Photo by Manya Saadi-nejad, reproduced with permission from Shohreh Mehran and MÉKIC Gallery, Montréal

Supreme Leader Ali Khamene'i. US policy toward Iran in the wake of the 2001 terrorist attacks on New York and Washington was not helpful. Rather than embracing Khatami's efforts at openness, in early 2002 US President George W. Bush branded Iran a member of the "axis of evil," even as Iran was quietly assisting the United States against al-Qaeda and the Taliban in Afghanistan. Bush's untimely declaration was taken in Iran as a deliberate slap in the face and undermined Khatami's support within the country.

Khatami was ultimately unable to push through any lasting changes because of opposition from conservative forces, and large numbers of reformists became disillusioned with his attempts to make Iran more democratic. Many boycotted subsequent local and national elections, allowing Supreme Leader Khamene'i's favored candidate, a working-class engineer named Mahmud Ahmadinejad, to win the presidency in 2005.

Under the populist and reactionary Ahmadinejad, the openness of the Khatami period steadily evaporated. Strict enforcement of women's dress codes was resumed, newspapers were closed, arrests and executions increased, and the West was once again painted as an irremediable enemy. Western politicians and media returned the favor by demonizing Ahmadinejad, seizing on his penchant for making provocative statements and often exaggerating or distorting them. For example, it became widely reported that Ahmadinejad had called for Israel to be "wiped off the map" as if this were some new official policy, whereas in actuality he had simply repeated Khomeini's prediction years before that one day "the Zionist regime will disappear from the pages of history."[8]

Ahmadinejad also alarmed and antagonized the West by ramping up Iran's nuclear enrichment program, which raised the specter of an Israeli attack or even a US-led invasion. Few leaders in the West considered such actions to be desirable, particularly given the failures of US-led interventions in Afghanistan and Iraq, but hawkish elements in both Israel and the United States aggressively pushed for war.

Though broadly disliked by the end of his first term both in Iran and abroad, Ahmadinejad was re-elected in 2009 under conditions that were widely perceived to have been rigged. Many held that the actual winner had been Mir Hossein Musavi, a mild-mannered architect who seemed at times almost reluctantly thrust into the limelight by his enthusiastic followers. Millions of Iranians poured into the streets to protest the election results, generating an apparently spontaneous phenomenon that came to be known as the "Green Movement."

The government responded with mass arrests of protesters and a wide range of known reformist figures suspected of sympathizing with them. Musavi and fellow candidate Mehdi Karrubi were placed under house arrest. A number of protesters were shot in the streets by security forces, as was an attractive young woman, Neda Agha Soltan, who was merely a bystander; her tragic death soon made her the poster girl for Green Movement supporters all over the world. Street protests continued to break out over the coming months, organized mainly through social media networks.

The government responded by busing militias of villagers into the cities and instructing them to attack the protesters, reportedly in exchange for kebabs and fruit juice. Thousands were arrested, and Karrubi used his website to bring to public attention the systematic rape of both male and female detainees in prison. According to one victim's account, "they did to me an act that is denounced even by unbelievers and idol worshippers."[9] (Responding to these allegations, then-president Mahmud Ahmadinejad admitted that rape and torture had occurred, but stated that they had somehow been carried out by enemy agents.) The Green Movement eventually disappeared from the streets, but its ideals continued to serve as a symbol of opposition and hope for change.

With these shaky beginnings, Ahmadinejad's second term was characterized by even harsher domestic policies and still more aggressive rhetoric toward the West. During this period, the Revolutionary Guards, with whom Ahmadinejad had close ties, bought up significant sectors of the Iranian economy, particularly in the oil industry and telecommunications. Iran's nuclear program dominated international policy toward Iran, leading to increased economic sanctions against the country. Most Western governments continued to press for a diplomatic solution to the impasse, but hawkish Israeli Prime Minister Binyamin Netanyahu, supported by right-wing elements within the US Congress, remained loudly adamant that military intervention was necessary to prevent a nuclear-armed Iran.

Iran's international isolation and stifling social atmosphere generated a considerable amount of cynicism during the Ahmadinejad period, especially among the younger generation who tended to be over-educated and under-employed. Sexual license and drug abuse were increasingly visible as expressions of rebellion and despair. Air pollution in the cities—exacerbated by the proliferation of vehicles constrained by sanctions to use inferior grades of gasoline—reached dangerous proportions, resulting in thousands of premature deaths. Universities were subject to tighter controls, with ideologically suspect professors being forced into retirement and "Western" fields such as the humanities being cut from many programs.

Amid growing international tension surrounding the nuclear issue, the election of a comparatively moderate cleric, Scotland-educated Hassan Ruhani, to the presidency in August 2013 was greeted with a sigh of relief by many both inside and out of Iran. Ruhani immediately softened Iran's position vis-à-vis the West, especially in regard to the country's nuclear program, but as his term progressed Iranians saw little in the way of change when it came to social freedoms, economic improvements, or democratic reforms.

The various crises and challenges Iranians faced during the last quarter of the twentieth century and into the twenty-first spurred an unending stream of migrations to more stable countries, particularly in Western Europe, North America, and Australia. Prior to the Iranian revolution in 1979, emigration from Iran had been minimal. The first Iranian expatriate communities in Europe and North America were established by individuals, usually from wealthy families, who went abroad to study and then stayed on, often taking Western wives.

The Iranian revolution, on the other hand, sparked a massive wave of out-migration, especially among the elite classes. Over a million ended up in southern California, which came to host the world's largest expatriate Iranian community. Others went to England, France, Germany, Canada, and Australia. In subsequent years large numbers of Iranians continued to leave their country, either for economic or political reasons or both. Most were highly educated professionals, representing a massive brain drain not seen since the sixteenth and seventeenth centuries when droves of talented Iranians sought better lives in India.

As was the case then, in Western countries today Iranian migrants have a very high rate of professional success and social integration. In North America they are statistically the second most highly educated immigrant group, after Germans. They tend to be overwhelmingly secular, unlike immigrants from other Muslim countries—Iranians having had perhaps too much of religion in public life, in contrast to other nationalities leaving home because they felt there wasn't enough.

The Iranian world has never recovered from the fragmentation it experienced in the eighteenth century. Afghanistan has remained a separate nation ever since Ahmad Durrani's declaration of independence in 1747, with its own modern history distinct from Iran's. The Tajiks living on the other side of the Oxus River to the north came to be part of Russian, then Soviet history, achieving statehood only in the late twentieth century. Kurds remain dispersed across Iran, Iraq, Turkey, Syria, and the Caucasus, their dream of an independent state still unrealized.

And yet, for many Persians, Afghans, Tajiks, Kurds, and others today—both at home and throughout the global diaspora—a strong emotive attachment to Iranian history and culture outweighs their formal citizenship. One is as likely to hear passionate recitations of the *Odes* of Hafez or Ferdowsi's *Book of Kings* in Kabul or Dushanbe (and increasingly in Los Angeles and Toronto) as in Tehran, and *Noruz* celebrations are invariably the highlight of the year wherever Iranians live. US President Barack Obama began giving an annual *Noruz* address in 2009, and in Canada it is a recognized holiday.

Noruz is unquestionably the greatest single event of the calendar year, not just for Iranian peoples including Kurds, Afghans, and

IRANIAN LANGUAGES TODAY

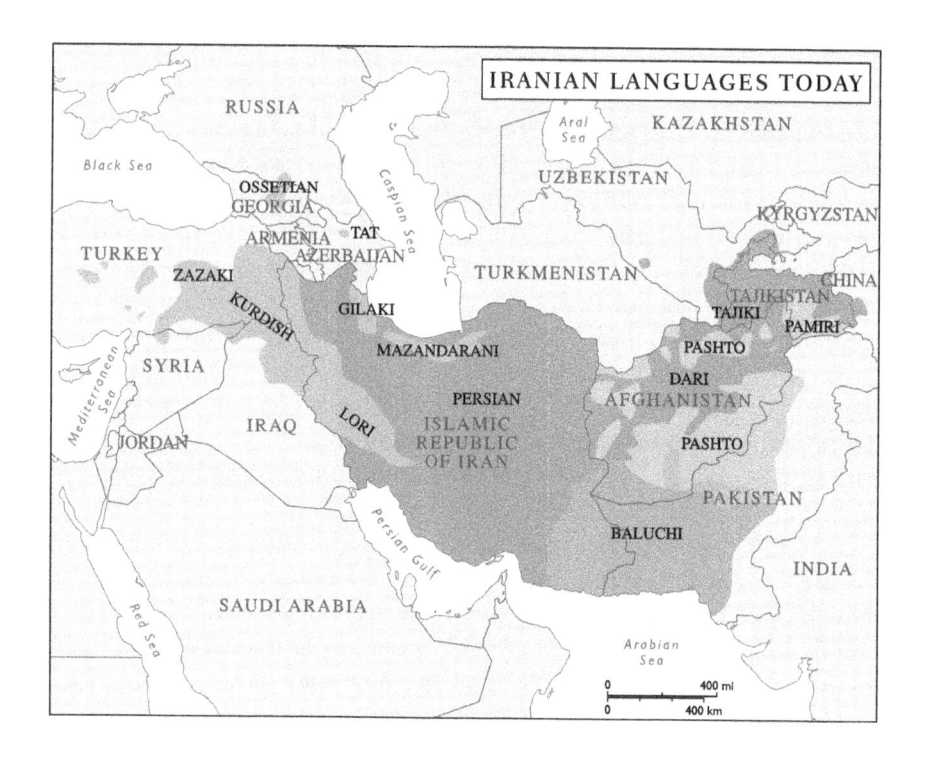

Tajiks but also many non-Iranians including Turkic-speakers such as Uzbeks and Kazakhs who consider it "their" national holiday. An echo of Mesopotamian myth survives within the now entirely secular and non-sectarian celebrations of *Noruz* itself, in the form of a trickster figure called Hajji Firuz who dances about and teases children. Hajji Firuz wears red (like the Christian Santa Claus), but his face is black, symbolizing his recent emergence from the world of the dead. The same symbol is connected with a number of young, handsome martyrs from Iranian mythology—for example, Siyamak and Siyavash from the *Book of Kings* (both names contain the word "black").

Unlike most Shi'ite rituals but in common with Zoroastrian ones, *Noruz* is a joyous celebration of life and family. All Iranians observe it, regardless of their ethnic or religious backgrounds. It is perhaps the single most unifying marker of Iranian identity. Sources from the early centuries of Islam provide numerous accounts of how Iranian Muslims continued to celebrate their "national holiday" alongside Zoroastrians, despite frequent opposition from the religious authorities. Entreaties by the likes of medieval theologian Mohammad Ghazali that *Noruz* should be "considered a simple, ordinary day like any other day and ignored"[10] went manifestly unheeded by the population at large.

In contemporary Iran as well, Islamic rule has had to accommodate the Iranians' love of *Noruz*, even certain aspects to which it objects. The Tuesday night before *Noruz*, called *Chahar-shanbe suri*, is a time when Iranians set bonfires and jump over them, speaking to the

The traditional New Year's spread (sofre-ye haft sin) features seven items that begin with the letter S: sabzeh (sprouts), samanu (pudding), sib (apple), serkeh (vinegar), sir (garlic), senjed (dried oleaster), and somaq (a fruity spice). The spread also typically includes other items such as a copy of the Qur'an, a mirror, and live goldfish. The Iranian New Year, Noruz, is the most important festival of the year and is celebrated by peoples from the Balkans to Central Asia and India. Photo by Manya Saadi-nejad fire: "May you take from me my yellow (that is, 'my fear'); may I take from you your red ('your courage and vitality')"—clearly an example of a very ancient ritual that has nothing whatsoever to do with Islam. The nationwide fire-jumping lasts for hours and is often accompanied by firecrackers and other chaotic expressions of joy and anarchy. With eighty million people simultaneously involved, it is impossible for Iran's security forces to maintain any semblance of public order during this wild and crazy evening.

Noruz is seen as a time of renewal, and Iranians typically spend weeks cleaning their homes in preparation for it. They lay out a special spread called *haft sin*, "seven [things beginning with the letter] S," which also includes a holy book (the Qur'an, the Avesta, or even the Odes of Hafez) and usually a bowl of water with live goldfish. There is also a plate of sprouts, symbolizing new vegetable life, which are kept till the thirteenth day of *Noruz*, called *Sizdah be-dar* (Thirteenth Outside), when they are taken out and cast into a body of flowing water such as a river or stream.

On the day of *Noruz* itself families sit together and count down excitedly to the moment of the equinox—even if it occurs in the middle of the night—and then rush into each others' arms with hugs and kisses to welcome in the new year. This event is followed by a two-week national holiday during which people visit each other's homes in turn, sharing tea, sweets, and conversation. It is a joyful time of year, but no business gets done. *Noruz* is perhaps the most visible sign of Iranian influence on neighboring peoples, being celebrated as a national holiday throughout Central Asia, the Caucasus, and as far west as the Balkans.

For much of history the Iranian world encompassed lands from Mesopotamia to the marches of India and China, even if the borders never remained fixed for very long. But if Iran is above all an *affinity*—an affective notion, rather than a political one—then borders are perhaps not what matters most.

Chronology

2000 BCE
Indo-Aryans occupy southern Ural region; begin southward migrations

1500 BCE
Indo-Aryan tribes split; some migrate southeastward over the Hindu Kush region and into the Indian subcontinent, while others (the proto-Iranians) move southward to the east of the Caspian Sea and onto the Iranian plateau

CA. 1200–1000 BCE (?)
Life of Zarathushtra (Zoroaster), founder of the Zoroastrian religion

881 BCE
First written mention of an Iranian tribe, the Medes, in Assyrian sources

678–549 BCE
Mede Confederation

549–330 BCE
Achaemenid Empire; conquest of Babylonia by Cyrus the Great, liberation of Israelites and other subject peoples; wars with Greek city-states; Alexander's conquests

312–62 BCE
Seleucid Empire; spread of Hellenism throughout Western and Central Asia and the northwestern Indian subcontinent; emergence of Graeco-Buddhist art

247 BCE–224 CE
Parthian Empire; competition with Romans; Iranian merchants dominate the Silk Road; contacts with China; spread of Mithraism throughout Roman Empire

224–651
Sasanian Empire; wars with Rome; codification of Zoroastrianism; Mazdakite movement

633–749
Arab conquests; Iranian lands come under rule of Syrian-based Umayyad dynasty; Iranian urban elites begin converting to Islam

749–51
Abbasid revolution; Iran-based revolt topples Umayyad Caliphate, shifts Islamic power base to Iranian world

751–1258
Abbasid Empire; Iranian cultural and political norms infuse the development of Islamic civilization; regional religio-cultural rebellions throughout Iran; Iranian Shi'ite Buyids dominate government of Islamic Caliphate

819–999
Samanid Empire in Central Asia; re-emergence of Persian as literary and administrative language

980–1010
Poet Ferdowsi redacts Iranian heroic epic *Shah-nameh* from various oral and written sources

977–1116
Ghaznavid Turkic Empire; lives of scholars Avicenna and Abu Rayhan Biruni; Turco-Persian Islamic culture introduced into India

1037–1194
Seljuk Empire; life of Sufi theologian Mohammad Ghazali; suppression of Shi'ism and reaction of Isma'ili assassins

1256–1335
Ilkhanid Empire; Mongol conquests, assimilation of Mongols to Perso-Islamic culture; lives of poets Jalal od-din Rumi and Sa'di of Shiraz

1370–1507
Timurid Empire; flourishing of literature and the arts, life of classical poet Hafez; fragmentation of empire into regional kingdoms

1501–1722
Safavid Empire; Iran forcibly converted to Shi'ism; apogee of Persian painting tradition; rise of Timurid Mughal Empire in India, attracting many Iranian migrants

1736–96
Khorasan-based Afsharid dynasty

1747
Foundation of Afghanistan

1760–94
Shiraz-based Zand dynasty

1796–1925
Ghajar dynasty; weak government, regions under control of powerful landowners; rise of European hegemony; rising Kurdish nationalism

1925–79
Pahlavi dynasty; modernization of Iran; Iranian-speaking Tajiks and Ossetes under Soviet rule

1978–80
Iranian revolution; Islamists led by Ayatollah Ruhollah Khomeini marginalize rival revolutionary groups and establish Islamic Republic

1980–88
Iran-Iraq war

1989
Death of Khomeini; pragmatist Hashemi Rafsanjani elected president

1997–2005
Reformist Mohammad Khatami is president of Iran

2005–2013
Conservative Mahmud Ahmadinejad is president of Iran

2013
Election of Hasan Ruhani as president of Iran

Notes

CHAPTER 1

1. Dse 2 (Darius's Susa fortification text, line 2), in Amélie Kuhrt, *The Persian Empire: A Corpus of Sources from the Achaemenid Period* (London: Routledge, 2007), p. 491. A similar inscription is found on Darius's tomb at Naghsh-e Rostam near Persepolis (DNa 2, in Kuhrt, *The Persian Empire*, p. 502). In another inscription at Bisotun, Darius boasts of being the first to put the "Aryan" language—i.e., Persian—into writing (DB 70, in Kuhrt, *The Persian Empire*, p. 149).
2. For Iranian loanwords in ancient Chinese, see Victor Mair, "Old Sinitic *M^yag, Old Persian Magus, and English 'Magician,'" *Early China* 15 (1990), pp. 27–47; on the possibility of Indo-Iranian elements in Japanese mythology, see Michael Witzel, *The Origins of the World's Mythologies* (New York: Oxford University Press, 2012), pp. 64, 83, 145, 150, 175, 285.
3. *Ābān Yašt*, 5:34, in Prods Oktor Skjærvø, *The Spirit of Zoroastrianism* (New Haven: Yale University Press, 2011), p. 114.
4. *Videvdat (Vendidad)*, 1.3 and *Bundahishn*, 28.47.
5. The *asvamedha* is described in *Rig Veda*, 1.162–3.
6. Thorkild Jacobson, *The Harps that Once . . . Sumerian Poetry in Translation* (New Haven: Yale University Press, 1987), p. 368.
7. His name means "camel-master," suggesting he likely lived in southern Central Asia at a time after the Iranian speakers had encountered the BMAC peoples. (Recall that the Iranian word for "camel" appears to have been borrowed from the BMAC language.)
8. *Yasna*, 49.4, in Skjærvø, *The Spirit of Zoroastrianism*, pp. 128–9.
9. *Second Book of Kings*, 18:11.
10. Herodotus, *The Histories*, 1.95–102.

CHAPTER 2

1. Isaiah, 45:13.
2. Irving Finkel, "Translation of the Text on the Cyrus Cylinder," www.britishmuseum.org/explore/highlights/articles/c/cyrus_cylinder_-_translation.aspx, lines 11–12.
3. Plato, *Epistles*, 7, 332b.
4. DZc 1 (Darius's Kabret inscription, line 5, from a granite stela in northern Egypt), in Kuhrt, *The Persian Empire*, p. 485.
5. Quoted in Paul John Frandsen, *Incestuous and Close-kin Marriage in Ancient Egypt and Persia: An Examination of the Evidence* (Copenhagen: Museum Tusculanum, 2009), p. 90.
6. Xenophon, *Hellenica*, 3.15.
7. Herodotus, *The Histories*, 4.116.2.
8. Diodorus Siculus, *The Library of History*, 17.70.4, 6.

CHAPTER 3

1. Plutarch, *Life of Crassus*, 24.5.
2. Fakhraddin Gorgani, *Vis and Ramin*, tr. Dick Davis (New York: Penguin Classics, 2008), p. 108.
3. From Mani's *Kephalaia*, translation in Iain Gardner and Samuel N. C. Lieu, *Manichaean Texts from the Roman Empire* (Cambridge: Cambridge University Press, 2004), p. 266.
4. From Kerdir's Pahlavi inscription on the so-called Kaaba of Zoroaster at Naghsh-e Rostam, near Persepolis.
5. *Greater Bundahishn*, 14A.0.1.
6. Abu Ja'far Muhammad b. Jarir al-Tabari, *The History of Al-Tabari*, Volume V: *The Sasanids, the Byzantines, the Lakmids, and Yemen*, tr. C. E. Bosworth (Albany: State University of New York Press, 1999), p. 298.
7. Abolqasem Ferdowsi, *Shahnameh: The Persian Book of Kings*, tr. Dick Davis (New York: Penguin, 2006), p. 682.
8. *Karnamag i Ardeshir Pabagan*, 2.11; tr. Raham Asha, *The Book of the Acts of Ardeshir son of Pabag* (Vincennes: Irman, 1999).
9. *Sad dar nasr*, no. 25, in Heinrich F. J. Junker, *Ein mittelpersisches Schulgespräcbt* (Heidelberg: Carl Winter, 1912), p. 20 (translation by author). I am grateful to Touraj Daryaee for alerting me to the existence of this little-known text.
10. *Sahih Bukhari*, no. 4425.
11. *Xin Tang Shu*, ch. 221, p. 6233.

CHAPTER 4

1. Abolqasem Ferdowsi, *Shahnameh: The Persian Book of Kings*, tr. Dick Davis (New York: Penguin, 2006), p. 833.
2. Ahmed b. Jarir Baladhuri, *Futuh al-Buldan*, ed. M. J. de Goeje (Leiden: Brill, 1866), p. 417.
3. Sulayman al-Qunduzi, *Yanabi al-mawaddah* (Ghom: Mehr Amir al-Mo'emin, 1384 [2005]), p. 419.
4. Nizam al-Mulk, *The Book of Government or Rules for Kings*, tr. Hubert Darke (London: Routledge and Kegan Paul, 1978), p. 236.
5. Qur'an, 33:21.
6. Montgomery Watt, *The Faith and Practice of Al-Ghazali* (London: George Allen and Unwin, 1953), p. 56.
7. Iftikhar Ahmed, *The Wise Sayings of Hasan al-Basri* (Mumbai: Tawhid Movement, 2013), p. 45, no. 80.
8. From the anonymous *Tarikh-e Sistan*, mentioned in C. E. Bosworth, "The Rise of the New Persian Language," in R. N. Frye, ed., *The Cambridge History of Iran*, Volume 4: *From the Arab Invasion to the Saljuqs* (Cambridge: Cambridge University Press, 1975), p. 595.
9. Quoted in Julie S. Meisami, "History as Literature," in Ehsan Yarshater and Charles Melville, eds., *Persian Historiography: A History of Persian Literature vol. X*, London: I. B. Tauris, 2012, p. 8.
10. Author's translation.
11. Author's translation.

CHAPTER 5

1. Abu Rayhan Biruni, *Alberuni's India*, ed. and tr. E. C. Sachau (London: Trubner, 1888), p. 17.

2. An Lushan's father died when he was young, and he was adopted by his mother's second husband who was of Parthian origin. His original Chinese family name was presumably Kang, meaning "Sogdian."
3. Nizam al-Mulk, *The Book of Government*, p. 179.
4. Omar Khayyam, *The Ruba'iyat of Omar Khayyam*, tr. Peter Avery and Jonathan Heath-Stubbs (New York: Penguin Classics, 2004), p. 47.
5. Jalal al-din Rumi, *The Masnavi: Book One*, tr. Jawed Mojaddedi (New York: Oxford University Press, 2004), p. 4.
6. *Golestan*, chapter 1, story no. 10. US President Barack Obama quoted the first two lines in his *Noruz* address on March 21, 2009.
7. In Persian sources the Timurids are referred to as "Gurgani."
8. Ibn Arabshah, *Tamerlane or Timur the Great Amir*, tr. J. H. Saunders (London: Luzac, 1936), p. 234.
9. Author's translation.
10. An Indian corruption of "Mongol"; though the Timurids were Turks, to Indian eyes any Central Asian invaders coming over the Hindu Kush mountains on horseback were considered "Mongols."
11. Zahir al-din Muhammad Babur, *Babur-nama*, tr. W. M. Thackston Jr. (Oxford: Oxford University Press, 1996), pp. 623–4.
12. Jahangir, *The Jahangirnama*, tr. Wheeler M. Thackston Jr. (Oxford: Oxford University Press, 1999), p. 77.
13. This breathtaking manuscript, which was acquired by American industrialist Arthur Houghton in 1959 and then dissected so as to sell off the individual folios, is referred to by some as the "Houghton Shah-nameh" and by others as the "Tahmasp Shah-nameh."
14. Wheeler M. Thackston Jr., "The Poetry of Shah Isma'il I," *Asian Art* (Fall 1988), p. 57.

CHAPTER 6

1. Tadeusz Jan Krusinski, *The History of the Late Revolutions of Persia* (London: Pemberton, 1733), vol. 2, p. 90.
2. Banafsheh Hejazi, *Tarikh-e hichkas* (History of Nobody) (Tehran: Qasidesara, 1385 [2006]), p. 79 (translation by author).
3. Sir John Malcolm, *The History of Persia, from the Most Early Period to the Present Time*, 2nd edition (London: Murray, 1829), vol. 2, p. 89.
4. Amin Banani, *Tahirih: A Portrait in Poetry* (Los Angeles: Kalimat Press, 2005), p. 12.
5. Joseph Wolff, *Travels and Adventures* (London: Saunders, Otley, 1861), p. 561.
6. J. H. Stocqueler, *Fifteen Months' Pilgrimage through Untrodden Tracts of Khuzestan and Persia* (London: Saunders and Otley, 1832), vol. 1, p. 118.
7. Mark Twain, "O' Shah," in *The Complete Humorous Sketches and Tales of Mark Twain*, ed. Charles Neider (Garden City: Doubleday, 1961), p. 377.
8. Mirza Malkum Khan, "The Law," in Charles Kurzman, ed., *Modernist Islam, 1840–1940: A Sourcebook* (Oxford: Oxford University Press, 2002), p. 113.
9. Quoted in Nikkie R. Keddie, *An Islamic Response to Imperialism: Political and Religious Writings of Sayyid Jamal ad-Din "al-Afghani"* (Berkeley: University of California Press, 1968), p. 171.
10. Quoted in Lloyd Ridgeon, *Sufi Castigator: Ahmad Kasravi and the Iranian Mystical Tradition* (London: Routledge, 2006), p. 23.

CHAPTER 7

1. Sadegh Hedayat, *The Blind Owl*, tr. D. P. Costello (New York: Grove Press, 2010), p. 1.
2. Nima Yushij, "In the Cold Winter Night," tr. Saeed Saeedpour, in *Modern Iranian Poetry* (Lincoln, NE: Author's Choice, 2001), p. 7.
3. Ahmad Kasravi, *On Islam and Shi'ism*, tr. M. R. Ghanoonparvar (Costa Mesa, CA: Mazda, 1990), p. 192.
4. Jalal Al-e Ahmad, *Gharbzadegi* [Weststruckness], tr. John Green and Ahmad Alizadeh (Costa Mesa, CA: Mazda, 1997), p. 11.
5. Quoted in Baqer Moin, *Khomeini: Life of the Ayatollah* (London: I. B. Tauris, 1999), p. 123.
6. From the poem "Sin," tr. Ahmad Karimi-Hakkak, in *Remembering the Flight: Twenty Poems by Forugh Farrokhzad* (Port Coquitlam, BC: Nik, 1997).
7. Ali Shari'ati, "Red Shi'ism (the Religion of Martyrdom) vs. Black Shi'ism (the Religion of Mourning)," www.iranchamber.com/personalities/ashariati/works/red_black_shiism.php.
8. Jimmy Carter, "Tehran, Iran Toasts of the President and the Shah at a State Dinner," December 31, 1977. Online by Gerhard Peters and John T. Woolley, *The American Presidency Project*, www.presidency.ucsb.edu/ws/?pid=7080.

CHAPTER 8

1. Ruhollah Khomeini, *Islam and Revolution*, tr. Hamid Algar (Berkeley: Mizan Press, 1981), p. 46.
2. R. W. Apple Jr., "Khomeini's Grip Appears at Its Tightest," *New York Times*, November 21, 1982, p. 28.
3. Quoted in Baqer Moin, *Khomeini: Life of the Ayatollah* (London: I. B. Tauris, 1999), p. 279.
4. Mohammad Hossein Mehrzad, "'I Have Always Been a Reformist and Against the Extremists': Interview with Faezeh Hashemi," *E'temad*, 28 Mordad 1392 [August 19, 2013] (translation by author).
5. Shirin Ebadi with Azadeh Moaveni, *Iran Awakening: A Memoir of Revolution and Hope* (New York: Random House, 2006), p. 204.
6. Robin Wright, *Dreams and Shadows: The Future of the Middle East* (New York: Penguin, 2008), p. 296.
7. Mohammad Khatami, "Our Revolution and the Future of Islam," in *Islam, Liberty and Development* (Binghamton, NY: Institute of Global Cultural Studies, 1998), p. 65.
8. See the discussion on Juan Cole's blog, "Ahmadinejad I Am Not Antisemitic," *Informed Comment*, June 26, 2006, www.juancole.com/2007/06/ahmadinejad-i-am-not-anti-semitic.html.
9. www.huffingtonpost.com/2009/08/25/mehdi-karroubi-publishes_n_268036.html.
10. Muhammad Ghazali, *Kimiya-ye sa'adat* (The Alchemy of Happiness), tr. Muhammad Asim Bilal (Lahore: Kazi, 2001), p. 695. Ghazali also states in this passage that it is forbidden for merchants to sell Zoroastrians the items they need for their ceremonies.

Further Reading

GENERAL WORKS

Arberry, A. J. *Classical Persian Literature.* London: Allen and Unwin, 1958.

Axworthy, Michael. *A History of Iran: Empire of the Mind.* New York: Basic Books, 2008.

The Cambridge History of Iran. 7 vols., various editors. Cambridge: Cambridge University Press, 1968–91.

Canby, Sheila R. *Persian Painting.* New York: Thames and Hudson, 1993.

Daryaee, Touraj, ed. *The Oxford Handbook of Iranian History.* New York: Oxford University Press, 2012.

Ferdowsi, Abolqasem. *Shahnameh: The Persian Book of Kings.* Trans. Dick Davis. New York: Penguin, 2006.

Foltz, Richard. *Religions of Iran: From Prehistory to the Present.* London: Oneworld Publications, 2013.

Ghirshman, Roman. *The Arts of Ancient Iran from Its Origins to the Time of Alexander the Great.* New York: Golden Press, 1964.

Potts, D. T. *Nomadism in Iran: From Antiquity to the Modern Era.* Oxford: Oxford University Press, 2014.

Potts, D. T., ed. *The Oxford Handbook of Ancient Iran.* Oxford: Oxford University Press, 2013.

Skjærvø, Prods Oktor. *The Spirit of Zoroastrianism.* New Haven: Yale University Press, 2011.

Yarshater, Ehsan, ed. *Encyclopaedia Iranica.* London: Routledge and Kegan Paul, 1982–89 and New York: Bibliotheca Persica, 1992–present.

IRANIAN ORIGINS: EARLY MIGRATIONS FROM CENTRAL ASIA

Anthony, David. *The Horse, The Wheel and Language: How Bronze Age Riders from the Eurasian Steppes Shaped the Modern World.* Princeton, NJ: Princeton University Press, 2007.

Kuz'mina, Elena E. *The Origin of the Indo-Iranians.* Leiden: Brill, 2007.

Mallory, J. P. and D. Q. Adams. *The Oxford Introduction to Proto-Indo-European and the Proto-Indo-European World.* Oxford: Oxford University Press, 2006.

Potts, D. T. *The Archaeology of Elam: Formation and Transformation of an Ancient Iranian State.* Cambridge: Cambridge University Press, 1999.

THE ACHAEMENID EMPIRE, 569–322 BCE

Briant, Pierre. *From Cyrus to Alexander: A History of the Persian Empire.* Warsaw, IN: Eisenbraun's, 2002.

Curtis, Vesta Sarkhosh and Sarah Stewart, eds. *The Idea of Iran,* Volume 1: *Birth of the Persian Empire.* London: I. B. Tauris, 2005.

Dandamaev, Muhammad A., and Vladimir G. Lukonin. *The Culture and Social Institutions of Ancient Iran*. Cambridge: Cambridge University Press, 1989.

Henkelman, Wouter F. M. *The Other Gods Who Are: Studies in Elamite-Iranian Acculturation Based on the Persepolis Fortification Texts*. Leiden: Nino, 2008.

THE SELEUCID AND PARTHIAN PERIODS, 322 BCE–224 CE

Curtis, Vesta Sarkhosh, and Sarah Stewart, eds. *The Idea of Iran*, Volume 2: *The Age of the Parthians*. London: I. B. Tauris, 2007.

Sherwin-White, Susan, and Amélie Kuhrt. *From Samarkand to Sardis*. Berkeley: University of California Press, 1993.

THE SASANIAN EMPIRE, 224–651 CE

Canepa, Matthew P. *The Two Eyes of the Earth: Art and Ritual of Kingship between Rome and Sasanian Iran*. Cambridge: Cambridge University Press, 2010.

Curtis, Vesta Sarkhosh, and Sarah Stewart, eds. *The Idea of Iran*, Volume 3: *The Sasanian Era*. London: I. B. Tauris, 2008.

Daryaee, Touraj. *The Sasanian Empire*. London: I. B. Tauris, 2009.

de la Vaissière, Étienne. *Sogdian Traders: A History*. Leiden: Brill, 2005.

Dignas, Beate, and Engelbert Winter. *Rome and Persia in Late Antiquity: Neighbours and Rivals*. Cambridge: Cambridge University Press, 2007.

THE ISLAMIC CALIPHATE, 651–1258

Crone, Patricia. *The Nativist Prophets of Early Islamic Iran: Rural Revolt and Local Zoroastrianism*. Cambridge: Cambridge University Press, 2012.

Curtis, Vesta Sarkhosh, and Sarah Stewart, eds. *The Idea of Iran*, Volume 4: *The Rise of Islam*. London: I. B. Tauris, 2009.

Daftary, Farhad. *The Isma'ilis: Their History and Doctrines*. Cambridge: Cambridge University Press, 2007.

Frye, Richard. *The Golden Age of Persia: The Arabs in the East*. London: Weidenfeld and Nicolson, 1975.

Herzig, Edmund, and Sarah Stewart, eds. *The Idea of Iran*, Volume 5: *Early Islamic Iran*. London: I. B. Tauris, 2011.

Hovanissian, Richard G., and Georges Sabbagh, eds., *The Persian Presence in the Islamic World*. Cambridge: Cambridge University Press, 1998.

LATER EMPIRES: THE IL-KHANS (1256–1335), THE TIMURIDS (1370–1507), AND THE SAFAVIDS (1501–1722)

Dale, Stephen F. *The Muslim Empires of the Ottomans, Safavids, and Mughals*. Cambridge: Cambridge University Press, 2010.

Manz, Beatrice Forbes. *Power, Politics and Religion in Timurid Iran*. Cambridge: Cambridge University Press, 2010.

Matthee, Rudolph P. *The Politics of Trade in Safavid Iran: Silk for Silver, 1600–1730*. Cambridge: Cambridge University Press, 2000.

Newman, Andrew J. *Safavid Iran: Rebirth of a Persian Empire*. London: I. B. Tauris, 2008.

THE FRACTURED EIGHTEENTH CENTURY: THE AFSHARS (1736–1796), THE ZANDS (1750–1794), AND THE FOUNDING OF AFGHANISTAN

Axworthy, Michael. *The Sword of Persia: Nader Shah, from Tribal Warrior to Conquering Tyrant*. London: I. B. Tauris, 2009.

Perry, John. *Karim Khan Zand*. Oxford: Oneworld Publications, 2006.

THE MODERN PERIOD: THE GHAJARS (1785–1925), THE PAHLAVIS (1925–1978) AND THE BRITISH-RUSSIAN SHADOW

Abrahamian, Ervand. *A History of Modern Iran*. Cambridge: Cambridge University Press, 2008.

Ansari, Ali. *Modern Iran*. Second edition. Harlow: Pearson, 2007.

Hopkirk, Peter. *The Great Game: On Secret Service in High Asia*. London: John Murray, 2006.

Kazemzadeh, Firuz. *Russia and Britain in Persia: Imperial Ambitions in Ghajar Iran*. London: I. B. Tauris, 2013 First published 1968 by Yale University Press.

Milani, Abbas. *The Shah*. New York: Palgrave Macmillan, 2012.

Mottahedeh, Roy. *The Mantle of the Prophet: Religion and Politics in Iran*. Second edition. Oxford: Oneworld Publications, 2008.

THE ISLAMIC REPUBLIC: 1979–PRESENT

Arjomand, Said Amir. *After Khomeini: Iran under His Successors*. Oxford: Oxford University Press, 2009.

Axworthy, Michael. *Revolutionary Iran: A History of the Islamic Republic*. New York: Oxford University Press, 2013.

Honarbin-Holliday, Mehri. *Becoming Visible: Women in Contemporary Iranian Society*. London: I. B. Tauris, 2013.

Kamrava, Mehran. *Iran's Intellectual Revolution*. Cambridge: Cambridge University Press, 2008.

Satrapi, Marjane. *The Complete Persepolis*. New York: Pantheon, 2007.

Sreberny, Annabelle, and Massoumeh Torfi, eds. *Cultural Revolution in Iran: Contemporary Popular Culture in the Islamic Republic*. London: I. B. Tauris, 2013.

Websites

Avesta—Zoroastrian Archives
www.avesta.org
An easily accessible, searchable repository of ancient Iranian texts translated into English. The site should be used with caution, since most of the translations are quite outdated and often inaccurate. It is nevertheless valuable as many of the texts are not available in any other English translation elsewhere.

British Institute for Persian Studies (BIPS)
http://bips.ac.uk
Mainly, though not entirely, concerned with archaeology; the institute's activities inside Iran were suspended after the revolution. Still, its site contains useful news of the field, information about research grants, lectures, workshops, and other Iran-related events (mostly in the UK), and access to the BIPS academic journal, *Iran*.

Circle of Ancient Iranian Studies
www.cais-soas.com
A repository of articles on pre-Islamic Iran, some scholarly and others less so.

Encyclopaedia Iranica online
www.iranica.com
Online edition of the primary scholarly reference for articles on Iranian history and civilization, edited by former Columbia professor Ehsan Yarshater.

Foundation for Iranian Studies
www.fis-iran.org
Offers a number of online resources, including an Iranian Oral History Project, an Iranian Women's Center, audio samples of Persian classical music, and archives of the Pahlavi dynasty.

Golha Project
www.golha.org
Extensive, searchable online database of music and poetry from Iranian radio programs.

Harvard (Ancient) Iranian Studies
www.fas.harvard.edu/~iranian
A very useful and reliable site run by Harvard Iranologist P. Oktor Skjærvø, including instruction in ancient Iranian languages, religions, and translations of texts not included in his published book *The Spirit of Zoroastrianism*.

International Society for Iranian Studies (ISIS)
www.iranian-studies.com
Official site for the US-based International Society for Iranian Studies, an organization of Iran scholars from all disciplines. Members can download articles from the association's journal, *Iranian Studies*, and find information about the biennial international conference.

Iran Chamber Society
www.iranchamber.com
A wide range of articles, many of them reprinted from other sources, on the history, art, and culture of Iran.

Iran Heritage Foundation (IHF)
www.iranheritage.org
The major international foundation supporting Iranian Studies as an academic field, IHF sponsors lectures, exhibitions, and cultural events, usually in the UK but sometimes internationally. Includes a searchable directory of Iran scholars worldwide.

Payvand
http://payvand.com
An English-language site for all things Iranian, including news, features, events, and a tool for converting Persian calendar dates to Western ones.

Sasanika
www.sasanika.org
Articles, resources, news, and events pertaining to Iran and its neighbors during the Sasanian period.

Shahnameh Project
http://shahnama.caret.cam.ac.uk/new/jnama/page
Worldwide database of manuscripts of the *Book of Kings*, including an electronic corpus of miniature paintings. Based at Cambridge University in the UK.

Tajikam—A Worldwide Community of Tajiks
http://tajikam.com/index.php
Articles on Tajik history, language, and culture, as well as current events and discussion forums.

Acknowledgments

As always, my thanks go first and foremost to my wife, Manya Saadi-nejad, who continues to motivate and inspire me to better understand her country and its history. She is my first and last resource for all things Iranian, and the recompense for all my efforts.

I am also grateful to Reza, Semiramis, Arya, Bardia, and Pasha Saadi-nejad, Azzam Sadati, Ruth Foltz, Shahrzad and Bijan Foltz-Navab, Persia Shahdi, and Camilla, Edmund, Adam and Susannah Brandt, for their love and for providing me with the extended family network that defines who I am. My father, Dr. Rodger Foltz, who passed away in September 2013 as I was beginning this project, was a central and vital part of that network and is deeply missed.

I would like to express my gratitude to Bonnie Smith and Nancy Toff, without whose encouragement this book might not have seen the light of day. Anand Yang, two anonymous reviewers, and two editors provided a wide range of helpful feedback—needless to say, I alone remain responsible for any errors of fact or interpretation.

I have been fortunate to spend the past ten years as a member of the Department of Religion at Concordia University in Montréal, which has proven to be the most supportive work environment any scholar could wish for. Our past three department chairs, Norma Joseph, Lynda Clarke, and Lorenzo DiTommaso, have been especially helpful in enabling us to bring Iranian Studies—a vital field that has fallen into a tragic state of worldwide neglect—into the Concordia curriculum.

Among the many people who have helped and encouraged me during the course of our frequent visits to Iran I would first and foremost like to thank my friend, mentor, and translator, Askari Pasha'i. The opportunity to benefit from his wisdom and erudition are always a highlight of my trips. I have had the pleasure of knowing many Iranians—family, friends, teachers, colleagues, students, and strangers—since I first began to enter their world nearly three decades ago, and most of them have contributed to my knowledge, understanding, and appreciation of their culture in some way or another. Any missteps or misperceptions stemming from these encounters are solely due to my shortcomings as a student of Iran's extraordinarily rich and complex civilization. *Agar khub nashod, bebakhshid!*

The New Oxford World History

GENERAL EDITORS

BONNIE G. SMITH,
Rutgers University
ANAND A. YANG,
University of Washington

EDITORIAL BOARD

DONNA GUY,
Ohio State University
KAREN ORDAHL KUPPERMAN,
New York University
MARGARET STROBEL,
University of Illinois, Chicago
JOHN O. VOLL,
Georgetown University

The New Oxford World History provides a comprehensive, synthetic treatment of the "new world history" from chronological, thematic, and geographical perspectives, allowing readers to access the world's complex history from a variety of conceptual, narrative, and analytical viewpoints as it fits their interests.

Richard Foltz is the Founding Director of the Centre for Iranian Studies at Concordia University in Montréal, Canada. His previous books include *Religions of Iran: From Prehistory to the Present* and *Religions of the Silk Road: Premodern Patterns of Globalization*.

CHRONOLOGICAL VOLUMES

The World from Beginnings to 4000 BCE
The World from 4000 to 1000 BCE
The World from 1000 BCE to 500 CE
The World from 300 to 1000 CE
The World from 1000 to 1500
The World from 1450 to 1700
The World in the Eighteenth Century
The World in the Nineteenth Century
The World in the Twentieth Century

THEMATIC AND TOPICAL VOLUMES

The City: A World History
Democracy: A World History
Food: A World History
Empires: A World History
The Family: A World History
Genocide: A World History
Health and Medicine: A World History
Migration: A World History
Race: A World History
Technology: A World History
Democracy: A World History

GEOGRAPHICAL VOLUMES

The Atlantic in World History
Central Asia in World History
China in World History
The Indian Ocean in World History
Iran in World History
Japan in World History
Mexico in World History
Russia in World History
The Silk Road in World History
South Africa in World History
South Asia in World History
Southeast Asia in World History
Trans-Saharan Africa in World History
Russia in World History

Index

Abadan, 108
Abbas I, 76–78, 80
Abbasid Empire, 49–50
Abd us-Samad Khan, 88
Abu Ali b. Sina. *See* Avicenna
Abu Hanifa, 52
Abu Muslim, 49, 50
Achaemenid Empire, xii, 1, 19, 20, 26, 33. *See also* Persian Empire
Adur Gushnasp temple, 42
Afghans, 76, 79–82, 88, 121
Afghanistan, xii, xiii, 4, 25, 26, 62, 64, 70, 76, 82, 88, 118–119, 121
Afshar tribe, 80
Agha Mohammad Khan, 84
Aghdashlu, Aydin, 105
Agriculture, 7, 19, 20, 66, 80, 87, 89, 102, 106
Ahmad Shah Durrani, 82, 121
Ahmad Shah (Ghajar), 93, 96
Ahmadinejad, Mahmud, 118–120
Ahrar, Khwaja Ubaydallah, 70
Ahura Mazda, *see* Mazda
'Ain Jalut, Battle of, 66
Airyanam Vaejo (Iranian mythological homeland), 1, 3
Akbar I ("the Great"), 73
Akhbari school, 79
Akkadian texts, 8, 16
Al-Azhar seminary, 64
Al-e Ahmad, Jalal, 102
Al-Qaeda, 118
Alborz Mountains, 11, 12
Alexander III of Macedon ("the Great"), 21, 24, 43, 82
Alexandria-on-the-Oxus, 26
Algerian Liberation Front, 106
Ali b. Abi Talib, 48, 52, 74, 76
Ali Beg Rumlu, 75
Ali Ghapu, 78
Allahverdi Khan Bridge, 78
Altai Mountains, 11
Americans, 103
Amir Kabir, 87
An Lushan, 61
Anahita, 2, 26, 31, 37, 44
Anatolia, xiii, 5, 14, 17, 19, 22, 25, 31, 33, 39, 61, 63, 67, 69, 74–75
Andronovo culture, 3, 5

Anglo-Afghan Wars, 88
Anglo-Iranian Oil Company (AIOC), 93, 100
Animation, 6
Angra Mainyu, 10
Ankara, Battle of, 69
Anshan, 7, 15, 16
Aq Qoyunlu. *See* White Sheep dynasty
Arab conquests, xii, 27, 33, 40, 45–46, 59
Arabic language, xiii, 55, 56, 58
Arabs, 45–47, 49; chauvinism of, 56
Aramaic language, 18, 19
Araxes River, 77, 95
Architecture, 69–70
Ardeshir I, 32–33
Armenia, 34, 63, 69
Armenians, 9, 31, 64, 77, 90, 92
Army, 19, 21, 22, 42, 61, 62, 63, 64, 77, 79, 81, 84, 88
Artabanus V, 32–33
Artaxerxes II, 26
Artillery, 75, 81
Aryan ideology, 98
Aryans, xiii, 1–2, 19
Assassins, 64
Assyrians, 7, 12, 14, 16, 20, 82
Astronomy, 67, 70
Asylum, 82
Atatürk, 96–97
Athens, 18, 21, 40
Attar, Farid od-din, 67
Augustine of Hippo, 35
Australia, 120–121
Avesta (Zoroastrian sacred text), 2, 10, 12–13, 36, 124
Avestan language, 10
Avicenna, 53–54
"Axis of Evil," 118
Azadi Square. *See* Freedom Square
Azerbaijan, 50, 67, 74–75, 86, 95; Soviet Republic of, 99

Bab, the, 86–87
Babak, 50
Baba Khan. *See* Fath Ali Shah
Babur, 71, 73, 75
Babylonia, 15, 25, 35
Babylonians, xiv, 18; Babylonian religion, 16

Backgammon, 6, 40
Bactria-Margiana Archaeological Complex (BMAC), 4–5
Bactrians, 19, 58
Badakhshan, 6
Badasht, 86
Baghdad, 50, 53, 55, 56, 62, 69
Baha'i faith, 86–87, 113, 117
Bahamas, 109
Baha'u'llah, 86–87
Bahram I, 36–37
Bahram II, 37
Bahram Chubin, 41
Bakhtiar, Shapur, 109
Bakhtiari tribe, 98
Baku, 80
Balkans, xii, 61, 123–124
Balkh, 56, 67, 82. *See also* Mazar-i Sharif
Baluch, xii, 82
Bandar Abbas, 78
Bani Sadr, Abo'l-Hasan, 113
Barbad, 4
Barbarian, 82
Barmak family, 56
Barmecides. *See* Barmak family
Barley, 4
Barzani, Mustaf, 99
Basij, 113
Bayazid I, 69
Bayazid Bistami, 55
Bazaar, 47, 78, 106
Bazargan, Mehdi, 110, 112
Behafarid, 49
Behbahani, Simin, 104
Behzad, Kemal od-din, 71
Behzadan. *See* Abu Muslim
Bible, 9, 13, 15–16
Bilingualism, 82–83
Biruni, Abu Rayhan, 60
Bishapur, 34
Black Friday, 108
Black Sea, 1
Black Sheep dynasty, 74
Blasphemy, 55
Bolsheviks, 93, 95–96
Book of Government, 64
Book of Kings, xii, 2, 42, 44, 45, 56, 58, 59, 63, 75, 121–122
Book of Righteous Viraz, 37, 46
Borandokht, 42
Borders, xi, 21, 124
Bozorgmehr, 40
Brain-drain, 76, 121
Britain, 92, 98, 100
British, 83, 87, 93
British Petroleum. *See* Anglo-Iranian Oil Company
British Raj, 60, 91, 115
Bronze, 3, 94

Bronze Age civilization, 4
Brothels, 79
Buddhism, xi, 12, 26, 35–36, 43, 67
Bukhara, xii, 56, 58, 63, 70, 81–83, 88
Bureaucrats, 33, 47, 56
Burial mounds, 3
Burnt City, 6
Bush, George W., 118
Bushehr, 83
Buyids, 62–63
Byzantines, 39, 41

Cafés, 79, 117
Cairo, 91
Cambyses II, 18
Camels, 5
Canada, 121
Cannes film festival, 116
Canon of Medicine, 53–54
Carpets, xi, 11, 27
Carrhae, Battle of, 29, 32
Carter, Jimmy, 107
Caspian Sea, 1, 4, 11, 66, 80, 86, 95
Cattle, 2, 4
Caucasus, 22, 25, 33, 61, 76–77, 83, 85, 121, 124
Central Asia, xi, xiii, 10, 13, 17, 19, 25, 27, 39, 43, 58, 60–61, 63, 68, 73, 81–82, 88–89, 123–124
Central Intelligence Agency (CIA), 100–102
Ceramics, 4
Chaghatay khanate, 68
Chahar bagh ("Quadrapartite Garden"), 27, 78
Chahar-shanbe suri ("Fireworks Wednesday"), 123–124
Chalderan, Battle of, 75
Chang'an, 43
Chariots, 3
Chess, 40
Children, 41, 56, 68, 86, 116
China, xii, 2, 11, 12, 32, 36, 61, 66, 68, 69, 77–78, 124
Chinese civilization, xiv; language, xiii; people, 32, 67
Chinggis Khan. *See* Genghis Khan.
Cholera, 89
Christianity, xi, 12, 31, 35–38, 43, 51
Christians, 52, 64, 67, 69, 77, 81, 113; monks, 55; persecution of, 31, 37; professors, 40
Cinema, 92, 116. *See also* Film
Circassians, 77
"Clash of Civilizations" theory, 117
Clergy, 53, 79, 86, 92, 97, 103
Cleopatra VII, 25
Coins, 12, 17, 19, 29, 31, 34
Cold War, 100
Colonialism, 87, 94, 106–107

Commerce, 19, 32, 43, 61, 67, 78. *See also* Trade
Concubines, 86
Conolly, Arthur, 88
Constantine I, 37
Constitutional Revolution, 92–93
Copper, 3
Cosmopolitanism, 19, 51
Cossack Brigade, 94
Cotton, 87
Coup d'état, 100–101
Cow, The (Mehrju'i, film), 104
Craftsmen, 2, 22, 33
Croesus, 17
Ctesiphon, 50
Cultural influences, xiv, 11, 12–13, 15, 21, 31, 45
Cultural synthesis, 5, 25, 26
Cuneiform, 8, 16
Cyrus II ("the Great"), 15–16, 18, 19, 24, 103; "Cyrus cylinder", 16, 17

Dabbagh, Hossein. *See* Soroush, Abdolkarim
Daghighi, Abu Mansur, 58
Damascus, 49, 50
Dancing, 79
Daqiqi. *See* Daghighi, Abu Mansur
Dar ol-fonun, 87, 91
Darband, 80
D'Arcy, William Knox, 93
Darius I, 1, 18, 19, 20, 21
Deeds of Ardeshir, 41
Delhi, 69, 73, 76, 81
Democracy, 97–98, 100, 106, 118
Derbent. *See* Darband
Devil, 13
Dialogue Among Civilizations, 117
Diba, Farah. *See* Farah, Empress
Diplomatic immunity, 103
Divine Comedy (Dante), 46
Divorce laws, 116
Donkeys, 5
Dragons, 2
Drug abuse, 120
Dunhuang, 43
Dura-Europos, 26, 30
Dushanbe, 57, 121
Dutch, 78, 80

Ebadi, Shirin, 116
Ebtekar, Massumeh, 117
Ecbatana, 16, 19. *See also* Hamedan.
Education, 40–41, 91, 97–98, 116, 120
Egypt, 19, 22, 25, 55, 62, 66, 105, 109
Elam, 7–8, 15
Elamites, xiv, 5, 7, 9, 18; Elamite civilization, 16, 93; Elamite language, 8, 19; Elamite religion, 8, 20

Elites, 23, 39–40, 47, 49, 56, 73, 98, 102, 106, 112, 121
Elizabeth II, 81
Engineers, 34, 118
England, 30, 41, 58, 73, 77, 84, 107, 121. *See also* Britain
English language, xiii
Esfahan, 64, 70, 77, 79–81
Esma'il I, 75–76
Esma'il II, 76
Ethnic cleansing, xiii
Euphrates River, 7, 26, 33
Europe, ix, xi, 2, 5, 11, 53, 54, 67, 70, 77, 78, 84, 89, 92, 96, 120

Famine, 39, 80, 89
Fanon, Frantz, 107
Farah, Empress, 104–105
Farhadi, Asghar, 116–117
Farman-Farmayan, Maryam ("Red Mary"), 100
Farmers, 22, 33, 39, 66, 102
Farrokhzad, Forugh, 104
Fars Province, 7, 83–84. *See also* Parsa
Farsi, *See* Persian language
Fath Ali Shah, 84–86
Fatemeh Baraghani, *See* Tahereh
Fatima bt. Muhammad, 48
Fatimids, 62, 63
Fedayin-e Khalgh, 107, 113
Ferdowsi, Abo'l-Qasem, xiii, 45, 59, 63
Ferghana Valley, 88
Fertility, 8, 115
Film, 92, 104. *See also* Cinema
Fin garden, 87
Fire worship, 10
Foucault, Michel, 108
France, 73, 84, 121
Freedom Movement of Iran (FMI), 107, 110
Freedom Square, 108
Fravahr (Zoroastrian symbol), 20, 22

Gambling, 79; closing of casinos, 108
Gambron. *See* Bandar Abbas
Gandhara civilization, 12, 26
Gardens, 26–27, 78
Gathas, 10
Genghis Khan, 66, 68
Georgia, 63, 69, 83–84
Georgians, 77, 92
Germany, 97–98, 121
Ghajar dynasty, 84–85
Gharbzadegi (Al-e Ahmad), 102
Ghashgha'i tribe, 98
Ghazali, Mohammad, 53, 55, 65, 122
Ghazan Khan, 67
Ghaznavid dynasty, 63
Ghazvin, 75, 77

Ghezelbash, 75–76, 80
Ghom, 97, 107–108
Ghorrat ol-'ayn. *See* Fatemeh Baraghani
Gilan, 95
Gnosticism, 35
Goats, 4
Goddesses, 8, 11, 20, 44
Goethe, Johann Wolfgang von, 84
Golden Horde, 68
Golestan. See Rose Garden
Golestan, Ebrahim, 104
Golestan, Treaty of, 85
Golshiri, Hushang, 104
Gondeshapur, 40
Gordian III, 33
Goths, 40
Graeco-Bactrian kingdom, 26
Greece, xi, 18; invasion of by Xerxes I, 22
Greek civilization, xiv, 12, 60; architectural styles, 17, 25; sculpture, 26; texts, 23, 25, 31
Greeks, 21, 26, 28, 34, 40, 61, 64; mercenaries, 22
Green Movement, 119–120
Gutians, 8

Hadith (report regarding the Prophet Muhammad), 49, 52
Hafez, 70, 83, 121, 124
Haft sin (Iranian New year's spread), 123–124
Haiku, 104
Hajji Firuz, 122
Hallaj, Mansur, 55
Halo, 26, 28, 44. *See also Khvaraneh*
Harem, 78–79, 90
Hasan of Basra, 53–54
Hasan of Tus. *See* Nezam ol-MolkHashemi, Faezeh, 115
Hazaras, 82
Hedayat, Sadegh, 98, 100
Hejab, 117. *See also* Veil
Hell, 3
Hellenism, 25, 26, 29, 51, 53, 61
Hephthalites, 39, 43
Heracles, 26
Heraclius, 42
Herat, 70, 82, 88
Heresy, 56, 76, 80, 86–87
Herodotus, 14, 21, 23, 24
Heroes, 2
Hezbollahi, 113
Hindi, 58
Hindu Kush Mountains, 82
Hitler, Adolf, 97
Hizbullah, 113
Holland, 73
Hollywood, 117
Homosexuality, 62, 117. *See also* Sodomy

Hormizd IV, 38, 41
Horses, 3, 8, 9, 11, 12, 20, 34, 62
Hospitality, 82
Hosseiniyeh Ershad, 107
Hostage Crisis, 112
Hülegü, 66
Humayun, 75–76
Humban, 8
Huns, 61
Hunting, 4, 24, 41
Huntington, Samuel, 117
Hurrians, 9
Husayn b. Ali, 48–49, 108

Ibn Muqaffa', 56
Il-khan dynasty, 66
Imperialism, 91
India, 10, 11, 12, 27, 40–41, 55, 60–63, 69–70, 73–76, 78, 83, 123–124
Indian civilization, xiv, 12
"Indian Mutiny", 91
Indian Ocean, 73, 78
Indo-European languages, xiii, 1–2
Indo-Iranian language, 3; Indo-Iranian religion, 10
Indo-Persian, xiii
Indus Valley, 6, 18, 25
Industrialization, 98, 101
Inscriptions, 1, 6, 9, 17–19, 26, 36
Intellectuals, 92, 98, 100, 108, 116
Iran-Contra scandal, 114
Iran-Iraq War, 113–114
Iraq, 48, 49, 71, 99, 103, 106, 113, 119, 121
Irrigation, 5, 7, 26
Ishtar, 20
Islam, 13, 43, 45, 58, 59, 117; conversion to, 47, 63, 64, 67, 73
Islamic Republic of Iran, xii, 111, 113, 116
Islamic Republic Party (IRP), 113
Islamic Revolution Guard Corps (IRGC), 110–111. *See also* Revolutionary Guards.
Isma'ilis, 64, 66
Israel, Kingdom of, 12; state of, 105, 119; invasion of Lebanon, 113
Istanbul, 64, 91

Jainism, 35
Jamal od-din "Afghani", 91–92, 102
Jamalzadeh, Mohammad Ali, 98
Jame' ot-tavarikh (Rashid od-in's universal history), 67
Jami, Abd or-rahman, 71
Jangali Movement, 95–96
Japan, 2
Jesus, 51
Jennings, Peter, 110
Jewelry, 4, 11, 22, 81, 85, 94

Jews, 31, 36–38, 52, 67, 81, 113
Jiroft culture, 5–6
Jonayd, 55
Judaism, xi, 26, 31, 35, 51
Judeo-Persian, 56
Justinian I, 40

Kaaba, 50
Kabul, 73, 82, 88, 121
Kadivar, Mohsen, 116
Kalila and Dimna (book of animal fables), 40–41, 56
Kandahar, 25
Karbala, Battle of, 48
Karim Khan Zand, 83
Karrubi, Mehdi, 119
Karun River, 7
Kartir. *See* Kerdir
Kashan, 7, 87
Kasravi, Ahmad, 99
Kassites, 8–9
Kavad I, 39
Kavad II, 42
Kazakhs, 24, 122
Kazakhstan, 11, 69, 88
Kerdir, 36–37
Khadijeh Soltan Daghestani, 81–82
Khalkhal Mountains, 96
Khamene'i, Ali, 114, 118
Khatami, Mohammad, 117–118
Khazars, 41
Khomeini, Ruhollah, 103, 106–108, 110–112, 114–116
Khorasan, 49, 53, 63, 75, 80
Khosrow and Shirin (Ganjavi), 42
Khosrow I, 39
Khosrow II, 41
Khosrow Parvez. *See* Khosrow II
Khotan, 12
Khubilai Khan, 68
Khvaraneh, 28, 33, 44. *See also* Halo
Khwarazm, 60, 62, 66
Kiarostami, Abbas, 116
Kiririsha, 8
*Komiteh*s (ad hoc neighbourhood militias), 112
Korea, 66
Krusinski, Tadeusz Jan, 80
Kuchik Khan, Mirza, 96
Kufa, 49
Kuh-i Nur diamond, 81
Kurdish Democratic Party (KDP), 99
Kurds, xii, 83, 96, 99, 121
Kushan Empire, 12, 31
Kyrgyz, 24

Lake Urmia, 9, 96
Landowners, 19, 39, 40, 62, 76, 87, 95, 98, 102

Latin, xiii, 54, 55
Law, 18, 75, 86, 91, 112
Layla and Majnun, 82
Lebanon, 76, 113–114
Linguistics, 1–2
London, 91
Lorestan bronzes, 94
Los Angeles, 121
Lost in the Crowd (Al-e Ahmad), 102

Magi, 13, 20, 36
Mahabad Republic, 99
Mahmud Ghilzai, 80
Mahmud of Ghazna, 60, 62
Majles, 92. *See also* Parliament
Malcolm, Sir John, 83
Malkum Khan, Mirza, 90–91
Mamluks, 62, 66
Mani, 35
Mania, 23–24
Manichaeism, 35–37, 43
Manzikert, Battle of, 63, 69
Marathon, Battle of, 18, 21
Marduk, 16
Marriage, 53, 67, 68, 81, 104; incestuous, 23
Martial law, 108
Martyrdom, 49, 55, 107, 122
Marv, 67
Marv, Battle of, 75
Mashhad, 97
Masjed-e Soleyman, 93
Masnavi-ye ma'navi (Rumi), 65
Massagatae, 17, 24
Maurya dynasty, 26
Mawali (client), 47, 48
Mazandaran, 94
Mazar-i Sharif, 82. *See also* Balkh
Mazda, 10, 20, 22, 36, 37
Mazdak, 39; survival of belief system, 50
Medes, 7, 9, 10, 11, 12–14, 15, 16, 17, 33
Mediterranean, 18, 33
Mehran, Shohreh, 118
Mehrju'i, Dariush, 104
Mental illness, 81
Mercenaries, 22, 24, 33
Merchants, 33, 36, 43, 44, 47, 48, 53, 56, 61, 78, 92, 97, 115
Mesopotamia, 3, 5, 6, 14, 22, 25, 36, 47, 75, 122
Mesopotamian civilization, xiv, 8, 19, 20
Mexico, 109
Migration, 1, 3–4, 7, 9, 37, 40, 60, 106, 120–121
Mirrors for Princes. *See* Wisdom literature
Mirza Hossein Ali. *See* Baha'u'llah
Misogyny, 37
Missionaries, 35, 64, 77, 80, 88–89
Mithraism, 26, 30–31
Modernism, 87, 91–92, 98, 102, 104

Mohammad Ali Shah, 93
Mohammad Bagher Majlesi, 79
Mohammad Khodabandeh, 76
Mohammad Reza Pahlavi, 98–100, 103–104, 107–109, 112
Mohammad Shah, 85
Mojahedin-e Khalgh (MEK), 107, 113–114
Monasteries, 43
Montazeri, Hossein Ali, 114
Mongolia, 2, 11
Mongols, 61, 66–68, 82
Moqanna', 50
Morocco, 109
Mosaics, 34
Mossadegh, Mohammad, 100–101, 107
Mourning rituals, 20, 49, 108
Mowlana. *See* Rumi
Mozaffar od-din Shah, 92–93
Mu'awiyah, 47
Mughal Empire, 73–76, 78, 81
Muhammad, 28, 43, 46, 49, 51, 53, 108
Muhammad Shaybani Khan, 75
Musavi, Mir Hossein, 119
Music, 42, 50, 62, 74, 79
Muslims, xi, 40, 47, 50, 60, 70, 89, 111, 122
Myths, 2, 37, 44, 122

New Year, 19, 20. *See also Noruz*
Nader Shah, 80–83
Naghsh-e Jahan Square, 77–78
Naghsh-e Rostam, 37
Najaf, 103
Nakisa, 42
Naqshbandi Sufi order, 70–71
Narseh, 37
Naser-e Khosrow, 64
Naser od-din Shah, 87–92
Naser od-din Tusi, 67
National Front, 107, 109
Nationalism, Iranian, 22
Nava'i, Ali Shir, 71
Navy, 78, 81
Netanyahu, Binyamin, 120
New York City, 118
Nezam ol-Molk, 64
Nezami Ganjavi, 42
Nicaragua, 114
Nishapur, 67
Nobel Prize, 104, 116
Nomads, 2, 5, 11, 22, 24, 33, 43, 61, 66, 69, 74, 80–81, 85, 89, 97–98
Noruz, 20, 52, 61, 121–124
Nose jobs (rhinoplasty), 117–118
Nostalgia, 58, 73
Nuclear program, 119–120

Obama, Barack, 121
Oil industry, 93, 100–101

Omar Khayyyam, 64–65, 84
Opium, 78–79
Oral transmission, 10, 32, 59
Organization of Petroleum Exporting Countries (OPEC), 105–106
Orthodoxy, 65, 74, 76
Oscar awards, 117
Ottoman Empire, 64, 69, 74–75, 77, 80, 87, 91, 93, 96
Oxus River, 121
Oxus temple, 25

Painting, 44, 71–73, 75, 84–85
Pakistan, xii, 71
Palestine, 15
Panahi, Jafar, 116
Panama, 109
Panjikent, 44
Paper currency, 67
Paradise, xi, 26–28, 49
Paris, 90, 98, 106, 108, 110
Parliament, 96, 112–113. *See also* Majles
Parsa, 7, 12, 32, 34. *See also* Fars Province
Parsumash, 7. *See also* Persians
Parthenon, 21
Parthian Empire, xii, 29–30, 33
Pasargadae, 17, 103
Patriarchy, 22–23, 37, 116
Pazyryk, 11
Peacock Throne, 81
Peasants, 19, 102
Persepolis, 19, 20, 21, 37; sack of, 24–25; 2,500-year celebration, 103–104
Persian Empire, 18, 19, 24. *See also* Achaemenid Empire
Persian Gulf, 78, 80–81, 83
Persian language, xii-xiv, 18, 19, 55, 59, 62, 64, 81–82, 97; revival of, 56, 58, 60
Persian literature, xi, 65, 70, 71, 104; Middle Persian, 56; translations into European languages, 84
Persian Soviet Socialist Republic, 95–96
Persians, 9, 11, 12, 14, 17, 26, 33
Philip the Arab, 33–34
Philosophy, 40, 51, 53, 79, 116, 117
Photography, 92
Pigs, 4
Pinikir, 8
Plague, 89
Plato, 18, 40
Plutarch, 29
Poetry, patronage of, 50
Pollution, 120
Polo, 40
Polytheism, 8, 10
Portugal, 73
Portuguese people, 27, 78, 80
Postal system, 19
Pottery, 3, 8, 27

148 INDEX

Prostitutes, 97
Protests, 103, 108–109, 119
Proto-Indo-European language, xiii
Ptolemy I, 25
Ptolemy of Alexandria, 70
Pushtuns, xii, 80, 82, 88. *See also* Afghans
Pushtunwali, 82

Qajar. *See* Ghajar
Qanat, 5, 19, 26
Qara-khanids, 63, 66
Qara Koyunlu. *See* Black Sheep dynasty
Qashqa'i tribe. *See* Ghashgha'i tribe
Qazvin. *See* Ghazvin
Qizilbash. *See* Ghezelbash
Qom. *See* Ghom
Qorrat ol-'ayn. *See* Fatemeh Baraghani
Quantum physics, xiv
Qur'an, 48, 51–52, 123

Radicalism, 104, 106, 112
Rafsanjani, Ali Akbar Hashemi, 115
Raiding, 2, 5, 8, 11, 41, 43, 46–47, 60–61, 63, 66, 73, 80, 89
Rape, 119–120
Rashid od-din Fazlollah, 67
Rasht, 80
Rastakhiz party, 106
Rationalism, 91, 99
Rayy, 84
Reagan, Ronald, 112, 114
Rebellions, 14, 15, 18, 41, 49–50, 61, 79, 81, 86, 95–96, 110
Reformism, 87, 90–92, 108
Registan Square, 73
"Regime change," 100
Resurrection, 13, 20
Revolutionary Guards, 113, 120. *See also* Islamic Revolution Guard Corps
Reza Shah Pahlavi, 94–98, 100
Reza Pahlavi, 104
Rhazes, 53
Rig Veda, 2, 3
Rokhshan. *See* An Lushan
Roman Empire, 35, 36, 37, 40, 42
Romans, 26, 28, 29–30, 32, 33, 38, 39
Rome, xi, 26, 29, 31, 33, 44
Romulus and Remus, 44
Rose Garden, 68, 84
Rostam, 59
Roxana, 24
Rudaki, 57–58
Ruhani, Hassan, 120
Rumi, Jalal od-din, 65, 67
Rushdie, Salman, 115
Russia, 66, 68, 78, 85, 95, 121
Russian language, xiii
Russians, 80, 83–85, 87, 93
Ruzbeh. *See* Ibn Muqaffa'

Sacrificial rites, 3, 10, 13, 20
Saddam Hussein, 113
Sa'di, Mosleh od-din, 67–6, 83–84
Safavid Empire, 74–77, 80–81, 83
Sakas, 11–12, 17, 18, 39, 61; women, 24. *See also* Scythians
Salman Farsi, 46
Samanid dynasty, 56–57, 63
Samarkand, xii, 43, 44, 49, 68, 69, 70, 73, 88
Sanctions, 115
Sanskrit, 2, 3, 10
Santa Claus, 122
Sarbedars, 107
Sari, 84
Sasanian Empire, xiii, 33, 35–41; conquest of, 46–47; Abbasid Empire as continuation of, 51
Satanic Verses (Rushdie), 115
Satrap, 16, 18, 25, 26
SAVAK, 102, 107
Savior, 13
Scythians, 11. *See also* Sakas
Sebuktegin, 62–63
Seleucid dynasty, 25, 26, 29
Selim I, 75
Seljuks, 63–64, 66, 69
Semitic languages, xiii, 18
Separation, A (Farhadi, film), 11
Sevruguin, Antoine, 90, 92
Sex-change operations, 117
Sexual license, 120
Seyyed Ali Mohammad. *See* Bab, the
Shah Murad, 82
Shah-nameh. *See Book of Kings*
Shah Rokh, 70
Shahr-i Sabz, 69
Shahr-e Sukhteh, *See* Burnt City
Shahsevan tribe, 98
Shamanism, 66, 74
Shapur I, 33, 35–36
Sharia, 51–52, 55, 112; abrogation of, 86
Shari'ati, Ali, 106–107
Sheep, 4
Sherley brothers, 76–77
Shi'ism, 48–50, 52, 62–63, 74–77, 82, 86, 99, 102–103, 107, 112, 116, 122; persecution of, 64, 80, 97
Shiraz, 7, 20, 27, 83–84, 86, 89
Shushan, 7, 8, 19. *See also* Susa
Shushtar, 34
Sibawayh, 56
Siberia, 1, 61
Silk, 77
Silk Road, xii, 29, 32, 36, 43, 44, 49, 56, 61, 73, 78
Simko Shikak, 96
Sintashta, 3, 5
Sizdah be-dar ("Thirteenth outside"), 124

Slaves, 25, 34, 53, 62, 80, 89
Smallpox, 87
Sodomy, 79. *See also* Homosexuality
Sogdians, 25, 32, 36, 43, 44, 49, 61; adoption of Persian language, 58
Sohrab, 59
Soltan Hossein, 79–80
Soltan, Neda Agha, 119
Soroush, Abdolkarim, 116
South Africa, 98
Soviets, 4
Soviet Union (USSR), 98–100, 121
Spain, 77
Spanish language, xiii
Spies, 88
Starvation, 80
Steppe culture, 1–3, 11, 24, 43, 66, 68; steppe art, 11
Stoddart, Charles, 88
Sufism, 53, 55, 65, 73, 75
Sugarcane, 87
Suicide, 116
Sultan Husayn Bayqara, 70
Sumerian texts, 8
Sunni, 52, 53, 62, 64, 68, 74–75, 81
Susa, 19. *See also* Shushan
Sweden, 117
Syncretism, 35
Syria, 12, 30, 47, 48, 53, 55, 69, 105, 121
Syrians, 34, 48, 58

Tabari, Abu Ja'far, 58
Tabriz, 66, 74–75, 85
Taghlid (following legal precedent), 91
Tahereh, 85, 87
Tahmasp, 75–76
Taj Mahal, 70
Tajikistan, xiii, 25, 44, 57, 64, 76, 121–122
Takht-i Sangin, 25
Talbot, Gerald F., 90
Taliban, 118
Talmud, 15, 51
Tamerlane, 81. *See also* Timur Barlas
Tammuzi, 20, 49
Tang dynasty, 32, 43
Tanzimat reforms, 87
Taqlid. See Taghlid
Tashkent, 88
Taste of Cherry, A (Kiarostami, film), 116
Taxes, 19, 30, 39, 47, 50–51, 64, 81
Tehran, 84, 88–89, 93, 107–108, 110, 114
Tehran University, 87
Tents, 11, 73
Tepe Sialk, 7
Terrorism, 108, 113, 118
Thousand and One Nights, 56
Tigris River, 7
Timur Barlas, 68–70. *See also* Tamerlane
Tobacco Revolt, 90

Tokharians, 12
Toronto, 121
Tower of London, 81
Trade, 30, 32, 43, 46–47, 70, 73, 77–78, 83. *See also* Commerce
Tristan and Iseult, 31
Tudeh party, 100, 113
Tughlugh dynasty, 69
Turanians, 59
Turkestan governnate, 88
Turkey, xi, xiii, 96–97, 103, 121
Turkification, 61, 63
Turkish language, xiii, 58, 61, 73
Turkmen, 69, 74–76, 89, 98
Turkmenistan, 4, 66
Turkomanchay, Treaty of, 85
Turks, 36, 41, 43, 60–62
Twain, Mark, 89
Twelfth Imam, 86, 103

Ulama, 52, 55, 75–77
Ulugh Beg, 70
Umayyad dynasty, 47–50
United Kingdom, 115. *See also* Britain, England
United States, 100–101, 106, 109, 112, 116, 118
Ural Mountains, 1, 3
Urartu, 9, 17
Urdu, 58
Usuli school, 79
Uzbeks, 71, 73, 75, 81–82, 122
Uzbekistan, xii, xiii, 4, 43, 66, 68, 76

Valerian I, 34
Vedic religion, 10
Veil, 64, 86, 97. *See also* Hejab
Velayat-e Faghih (Guardianship of the Jurist), 112, 116

Warriors, 2, 61, 62, 63, 68–69, 76
Washington, DC, 118
West (the), xi; Westerners, xi; Western culture, xi; Western hegemony, xi; Western media, xii; Westernization, 97–98, 102
Wheat, 4, 5, 106
White Balloon, The (Panahi, film), 116
White Huns. *See* Hephthalites
"White Revolution," 102–103
White Sheep dynasty, 74
Wisdom literature, 40
Wolff, Joseph, 88
Women, 23, 56, 64, 79, 90, 97–98, 100, 115–16; enforcement of dress codes, 119; inability to rule; Mazdakite view of, 39; sexuality, 37; suffrage, 102–103
World War I, 64, 93, 96

150   INDEX

Xenophon, 24
Xerxes I, 21, 22
Xian. *See* Chang'an
Xinjiang, 12

Yaqub b. Layth, 56
Yazdegerd III, 42, 46
Yom Kippur War, 105
Yushij, Nima, 98–99

Zab River, 49
Zagros Mountains, 4, 7, 12

Zahedi, General Fazlollah, 100
Zarathushtra, *see* Zoroaster
Zayandeh River, 77–78
Zeus, 26
Ziggurat, 6–9
Zoroaster, 9–10
Zoroastrianism, xi, 13, 19–20, 22, 26–27, 35, 36, 39, 49, 122
Zoroastrians, 10, 22, 36, 81, 113, 122